KEEPING QUAIL

A guide to domestic and commercial management

Katie Thear

Broad Leys Publishing

Keeping quail: a guide to domestic and
commercial management
First edition: 1987
Copyright © 1987. Katie Thear
Typeset by Christine Challinor
Printed and bound by Whitstable Litho Ltd.,
Whitstable, Kent CT5 3PP.
Published by Broad Leys Publishing Co.,
Widdington, Saffron Walden, Essex CB11 3SP.

BRITISH LIBRARY CATALOGUING IN PUBLICATION DATA
Thear, Katie
Keeping Quail: A Guide to Domestic and Commercial Management
1. Quails
1. Title
636.5'9   SF510.Q2
ISBN 0–906137–15–2

Details of publications produced by Broad Leys Publishing are available by
writing or telephoning for a complete list to Broad Leys Publishing Co.,
Widdington, Saffron Walden, Essex CB11 3SP. Telephone: Saffron Walden
(0799) 40922.

Contents

Male Coturnix laying quail in an outside breeding pen.

Introduction

The keeping of quail has tended to be rather a grey area as far as availability of information is concerned. This is possibly because comparatively few people have kept them in the past, although currently there is a considerable degree of interest in these productive little birds.

I began to keep quail nearly ten years ago and in that time my interest in them has never palled. It must be admitted that I learned a great deal by trial and error, and in this respect, I hope that my experiences will prove useful to those contemplating keeping quail for the first time. While researching the subject, initially for my own interest, and subsequently for this book, I have met and talked to many quail breeders, amateur and professional, in this country and abroad. Their enthusiasm, knowledge and support have been major incentives to sitting down and writing the book.

Quail are classified as game birds, sharing the same family as pheasants and partridges. Although there are over forty different species of quail in the world, the number of species kept domestically or commercially, or as ornamental aviary birds, is quite small. The book concentrates, therefore, on the breeding and management of those species, notably the Coturnix laying strains, the Bobwhite meat breeds, and the ornamental aviary breeds such as the Chinese Painted quail. However, the book does not neglect the wider scale in relation to overall breed development and diversification in different parts of the world.

My hope is that readers will find the book useful and helpful in a practical context. If you feel that I have neglected any particular aspect of the subject, please write and let me know so that any suggestions may be incorporated in future editions.

Katie Thear
Widdington, 1987

Fawn variety of Coturnix laying quail (see also the photograph on the outside front cover).

History of quail

The earliest known representation of the quail is in Egyptian hieroglyphics, when the little bird was presumably common enough and important enough to merit a place in the alphabet. It is not known what the breed development has been over the centuries, but there are two closely related species in the wild, the Common or European quail, *Coturnix coturnix*, and the Eurasian or Pharoah quail, *Coturnix communis*. The chances are that these were both derived from a common source in the past. In the Americas, there is a quite different strain in the Bobwhite quail, *Colinus species,* and worldwide, there are thirteen other sub-groupings of quail.

Remains of the Coturnix quail have been found in Upper Pleistocene rocks in Britain, notably in Chudleigh Cave and Kent's Cave in Devon, Hoe Grange Cave in Derbyshire and Kirkdale Cave in Yorkshire.

In the Bible, there is reference to how food was brought to the starving Israelites in the wilderness: *'There went forth a wind from the Lord and brought quails from the sea.'*

Quail are mentioned in the eighth century Saxon writings, and later by the poet John Clare in his bird listings for East Anglia in the seventeenth century.

Beethoven utilized the call of the quail (*wet-my-lips*) in his music. See if you can spot it in his Pastoral Symphony!

In 1859, Mrs. Beeton had this to say:

'Quails are almost universally diffused over Europe, Asia and Africa, in the autumn, and returning again in the spring, frequently alighting in their passage on many of the islands of the Archipelago, which, with their vast numbers, they almost completely cover.....It appears highly probable that the quails which supplied the Israelites with food during their journey through the wilderness, were sent by a wind from the south-west, sweeping over Egypt and Ethiopia towards the shores of the Red Sea. In England they are not very numerous,

7

Early representations of the quail

Painted relief from the tomb of Seti 1, Thebes.

Section of the Hunefer papyrus scroll

Reliefs from the Temple of Seti 1, Abydos.

Woodcut from Mrs Beeton's Book of Household Management, 1861.

Woodcut from Thomas Bewick's History of Birds, 1820.

Some of the author's quail. Left to right: Tuxedo variety of Coturnix quail Bobwhite and Fawn variety of Coturnix.

although they breed in it; and many of them are said to remain throughout the year, changing their quarters from the interior parts of the country for the seacoast.'

Sir Herbert Maxwell reported that ,*'there was a moderate immigration in 1893'* and commented that *'the fecundity of the species must be prodigious; millions being taken in nets during their spring and autumn migrations across the Mediterranean.'* These, he claimed, went to the *'great cities of Europe, where hundreds of thousands are consumed at the tables of wealthy persons.'*

The quail is the state bird of California. On a recent visit to the USA, I was entranced to see a group of the attractive little California quail,*Lophortyx californica*, on the edge of lake Cachuma.

In recent years, a considerable quail industry has grown in the United States, Japan, Italy, France and Britain. This is to cater for the gourmet interest in quail's eggs and delicatessen table birds. In Japan, the quail also has the dubious distinction of being bred for laboratory testing.

9

About the quail

There is a wide variety of breeds which have become adapted to varying climates and conditions. In this brief look at the characteristics of quail, it is only possible to concentrate on generalities of the more common breeds, and to give a few personal observations.

Most quail are birds of the undergrowth which, depending on breeds and geographical distribution, may be tall grasses, dense bush, shrub thickets, overgrown fields, meadows, plantations or savannahs. They are essentially shy retiring birds which will 'quail' with fear into the shadow and security of the undergrowth. When really disturbed however, they will break cover like pheasants, and fly straight up into the air with a characteristic whirring of wings.

Most are ground-orientated in that they spend most of their time on the ground in the wild, except when they are migrating or disturbed in some way. Some are more ground-orientated than others. The Chinese Painted quail, for example, is like a small mouse scuttling about on the ground, resorting to occasional short flights where necessary. The Bobwhite, by comparison, likes to fly and perch.It is important, therefore, to make adequate provision for such behaviour within an aviary system. Clumps of grass or shrubs are needed to provide cover, while a couple of branches enable perching to take place.

Most breeds of quail have long toes and claws, an adaptation for scratching for insectivorous foods. In an aviary there is usually provision for this but if, for example, they have only a concrete run, do make sure they have an area where fine soil or sand can be made available for scratching purposes. In cages other than battery ones, they will appreciate wood shavings or sand for the same purpose, as well as for absorbing droppings. In a battery cage system, this is not possible, and it is one of the reasons why I dislike the battery system for any bird or poultry, because it does not provide conditions for them to exercise their natural instincts.

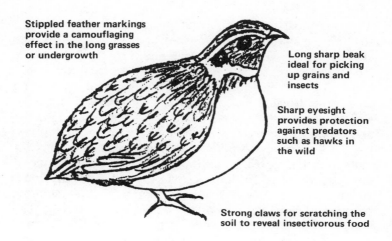

Stippled feather markings provide a camouflaging effect in the long grasses or undergrowth

Long sharp beak ideal for picking up grains and insects

Sharp eyesight provides protection against predators such as hawks in the wild

Strong claws for scratching the soil to reveal insectivorous food

The quail's beak is long, pointed and sharp, ideally suited for pecking small insects, grains or for shredding small pieces of vegetation. It can also be an aggressive weapon if one quail decides to attack another. In my experience, it is usually a male which attacks in this way, often attacking another male in the breeding season. For this reason, as well as avoiding unwanted cross-breeding, it is a good idea to keep the males separate. Again, there are exceptions and on a small-scale where there is less pressure of numbers and general stress, they may live together quite happily. I have seven different breeds of quail and they share the same aviary and concrete run in the summer, with occasional browsing periods on grass in a movable run. (See page 39.) In winter, the breeding stock is housed in canary breeding cages in the conservatory (see page 45) but are frequently released to enjoy the freedom of the conservatory. I have only found one Coturnix male to be aggressive in these conditions, and as a result, he stays in his cage, enviously watching the others parading up and down the conservatory.

I do not let them inter-breed of course. When I want to collect eggs for incubation purposes, I confine the male and females of a particular breed together and keep them separate from the others until I can be sure that the eggs are pure.

I must emphasize that my birds may be demonstrating behaviour different from the norm, because they are so tame. They know me and are used to being stroked, talked to and will often take food from my hand. On sunny winter days, I often work at my writing at a table in the conservatory. One or more of the quail will fly up and see what I'm doing, often settling down and going to sleep a few inches away. The photograph on page 13 shows an American Range quail on the table, a regular inspector of what I'm scribbling. As a matter of interest, there is an American book called 'That Quail, Robert', by Margaret Stranger which is a fascinating account of how the author tamed a Bobwhite quail. The copy I read was borrowed from the local library, and details are given in the reference section.

On a commercial scale, this kind of relationship is not possible with what is regarded purely as stock, and there is no reason why it should be if the main concern is to acquire the maximum number of eggs or to produce table birds. Even on a commercial scale however, I would not condone the barbaric practice of beak clipping in order to reduce the incidence of pecking. This is usually the result of over-crowding and boredom.

The question is often asked — how noisy are quail? As with all things, only a relative answer is possible. As a generalization, males are noisier than females, which confine themselves to subdued little chirrups and soft 'tic-tics' or cooings. The male Coturnix has a rasping chirruping crow, rather like the harsh cry of the magpie, and is altogether louder and more penetrating. The photograph on page 14 shows a Tuxedo Coturnix male adopting the characteristic upright stance and open-beaked expression when letting the world know of his whereabouts.

The Bobwhite male is also loud, but I do not find his call quite as aggravating as that of the Coturnix. It is basically a three-note, full-bodied piping sound. The female has a quieter version of the same call, with more of a tendency to chirrup.

The Chinese Painted male has a melodious, rather wistful piping whistle. It is almost minor-key, with an evocative atmosphere of the jungle in it. The female is

American Range variety of Coturnix quail. Note the large feet in comparison with its size, adapted for scratching the earth for insectivorous food.

quiet, apart from the occasional and busy 'chic-chic' as she darts about looking for insects.

Finally, I should mention the tendency of Coturnix quail to fly straight up and dash their heads on the roof, sometimes causing injury. It is apparent all through the year, but is much more so in the period leading up to the breeding season, when the migratory urge is at its peak. The only way to deal with this is to place netting just below the roof so that they do not hurt themselves. Further details are given on page 43.

Tuxedo variety of Coturnix laying quail. Note the upright stance of the male when calling.

Breeds

If we 'place' the quail in its relative position in the bird world, it is found in the order of *Galliformes*. This is a group which includes game birds and domestic fowl, but not waterfowl. Narrowing the classification further, it is a member of the *Phasianidae* family, a category it shares with pheasants and partridges.

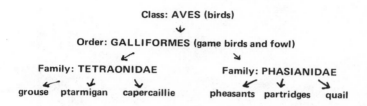

Class: AVES (birds)

Order: GALLIFORMES (game birds and fowl)

Family: TETRAONIDAE

grouse   ptarmigan   capercaillie

Family: PHASIANIDAE

pheasants   partridges   quail

Within the quail group, there are fourteen sub-groupings, as indicated:

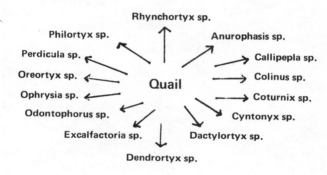

Rhynchortyx sp.

Philortyx sp.   Anurophasis sp.

Perdicula sp.   Callipepla sp.

Oreortyx sp.   Colinus sp.

Ophrysia sp.   Quail   Coturnix sp.

Odontophorus sp.   Cyntonyx sp.

Excalfactoria sp.   Dactylortyx sp.

Dendrortyx sp.

Each of these sub-groupings has one or more representative species, as shown, and some of these species have sub-species in turn, demonstrating the genetic diversification in different geographical locations:

There are over forty species of quail in the world, with more than twenty currently being bred in captivity. The Quail Group of The World Pheasant Association has an on-going survey of what breeds are being bred, recordings which are most valuable in relation to conservation work in this field.

Sub-groupings of quail

Anurophasis monorthonyx		— Snow Mountain quail
Callipepla californica (Lophortyx californica)		— Californian quail
	C. douglasii	— Elegant quail
	C. gambelii	— Gambel's quail
	C. squamata	— Scaled quail
Colinus cristatus		— Crested Bobwhite quail
	C. nigrogularis	— Blackthroated Bobwhite quail
	C. virginianus	— Bobwhite quail
Coturnix coromandelica		— Rail quail
	C. coturnix (C. communis)	— Common, European, Eurasian or Pharoah quail
	C. delegrouei	— Harlequin quail
	C. japonica	— Japanese quail
Cyntonyx montizumae		— Mearns quail
	C. ocellatus	— Ocellated quail
Dactylortyx thoracicus		— Singing quail
Dendrortyx barbatus		— Bearded Tree quail
	D. leucophrys	— Buffycrowned Tree quail
	D. macroura	— Longtailed Tree quail
Excalfactoria chinensis		— Chinese Painted quail
Odontophorus atrifrons		— Blackfronted Wood quail
	O. balliviani	— Stripefaced Wood quail
	O. capueira	— Spotwinged Wood quail
	O. columbianus	— Venezualan Wood quail
	O. dialencos	— Tacaruna Wood quail
	O. erythrops	— Rofousfronted Wood quail
	O. gujanensis	— Marbled quail
	O. guttatus	— Spotted Wood quail
	O. hyperythrus	— Chestnut Wood quail
	O. leucolaemux	— Whitethroated Wood quail
	O. melanonotus	— Darkbacked Wood quail
	O. speciosus	— Rufousfronted Wood quail
	O. stellatus	— Starred Wood quail
	O. strophium	— Gorgeted Wood quail
Ophrysia superciliosa		— Indian Mountain quail
Oreortyx picta		— Mountain quail
Perdicula argoondah		— Rock Bush quail
	P. asiatica	— Jungle Bush quail
	P. erythrorhyncha	— Painted Bush quail
	P. manipurensis	— Manipur Bush quail
Philortyx fasciatus		— Banded quail
Rhynchortyx cinctus		— Tawnyfaced quail

The table above shows the fourteen sub-groupings of the quail family. Each one , such as Coturnix, Colinus or Oreortyx, has one or more species. These, in turn, may have their own sub-species, such as different colour varieties.

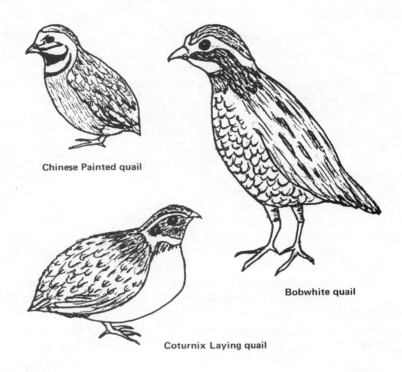

Chinese Painted quail

Bobwhite quail

Coturnix Laying quail

Quail vary in size, from the largest, **Longtailed Tree quail**, *Dendrortyx macroura*, at nearly 14", to the smallest, **Chinese Painted quail**, *Excalfactoria chinensis*, at just over 4". They are found in a wide range of climates, but all share similar characteristics of being shy, quick and with a tendency to hide in ground cover such as long grass or other vegetation.

Domesticated breeds

The word 'domesticated' is used advisedly, for no breed of quail is domesticated in the sense that domestic fowl have been developed. They are still essentially 'wild' in their form and behaviour. Although selective breeding has taken place to produce egg laying strains or birds more suited to the table, the development is nowhere near as marked as it is with domestic fowl.

Coturnix laying quail

This is the most common type in captivity world-wide. It is essentially the same bird that the Ancient Egyptians knew and which Mrs. Beeton would have recognised as one of the *'feathered game which have from time immemorial given gratification to the palate of man'*. When reference is made to 'quail' in general, this is the bird in question. In Europe, it has been known as **Common** quail, **European** quail and **Mediterranean** quail. The Old English country name was **Wet-my-lips**, a reference to its familiar call. **Pharoah's** quail is linked with its Egyptian origins, while in the USA, early settlers referred to it as **German** quail, no doubt because German settlers brought it with them. **Eurasian** quail is a reminder of its considerable geographical distribution.

No-one can know for certain exactly how the various breeds and sub-species developed, but it is generally acknowledged that the Coturnix types are based on the **Common European** quail, *Coturnix coturnix*, **Pharoah** or **Eurasian** quail, *Coturnix communis*, and more recently, **Japanese quail**, *Coturnix japonica* . This was first recognised in the nineteenth century as a separate breed in the wild, but in recent years, the Japanese have developed more productive commercial strains which are also called **Japanese quail**. Selectively bred laying strains developed from *C. coturnix, C. communis* and *C. japonica,* are often impossible to distinguish. For convenience, it is easier to refer to them merely as **Coturnix laying quail**. In America however, they tend to call Coturnix layers, **Pharoah quail**. In Japan they understandably call them **Japanese quail**. In Britain where, as always we compromise to try and keep everyone happy, we call them all these things. It can be most confusing!

They are basically the same: The male grows to a maximum of 6½", while the female is slightly larger at an average of 7½". Both sexes have dappled dark brown, buff and cream striated backs, paler underbellies, breast and flanks. In the female, the markings are less pronounced, while the male's chest is reddish brown. This particular feature enables sex identification to take place at around 3 weeks of age. Before then, it is extremely difficult to do so.

In both sexes there is a distinctive light stripe above each eye, and a white collar, although these may be diminished or even lacking in the female. The beak is yellow-brown to dark olive-brown, the legs pinkish-yellow and the eyes dark brown.

The Coturnix laying quail (whether called Japanese or Pharoah) has been selectively bred for commercial production to a limited extent, and the breeders have, in turn, given their own names to particular strains. In the UK, for example, Curfew have developed their own **Crusader** strains, while in the USA, Marsh Farms have produced their own **Marsh Pharoah** strains.

Coloured varieties of Coturnix quail

As well as the normal or commercial type of Coturnix laying quail, there are several varieties which show distinct colour variations and markings. The most common are as follows:

Manchurian quail: The alternative name for these is Manchurian Golden because of their colouring. They are essentially the same breed as the Japanese or Pharoah, but have been developed as a separate variety with golden colouring. Although the markings are essentially the same, the overall hue is lighter and more golden.

American Range: The overall colouring is dark brown, so that some people refer to them as **Brown** quail. This is a mistake however, for the Brown quail is the name normally given to the Australian breed, *Synoicus ypsilophous*, which is bigger and more greyish in appearance. However, there is a similarity and it is certainly possible that the early Australian settlers introduced the Common quail to that Continent, with subsequent isolated development producing apparently different species.

The markings of the American Range are essentially a lighter brown body colour overlaid with darker-brown, almost black pencilling, along with a certain amount of dark grey feathering on the back. The latter is a point of comparison with the Australian Brown quail.

English White variety of the Coturnix laying quail.

In America, the Range Coturnix is referred to as the **British Range**, while in the UK, we call it the **American Range**. (It must mean something.)

The overall appearance is dark-brown while the striped head markings are similar to other Coturnix breeds. However, the white eyebrow stripe and white throat markings are absent. Beak and legs are olive-brown and eyes, dark brown.

Fawn quail: This is the variety shown on the outside front cover and is one of my favourites. Essentially like all the other Coturnix breeds, the overall impression of the Fawn is a lovely warm pinkish-brown. The fawn feathers are pencilled with white and the white eyebrow lines are present, although not as strongly defined as in other breeds. Beak and legs are light pinkish-brown, while the eyes are dark brown.

There is no colour difference between the sexes, although as in other breeds, the female is slightly bigger than the male.

English White: Good specimens of these are completely white, with no discernible markings, other than the merest hint of eyebrow lines on the head. It is common, however, to have odd patches of black, and a look at the photograph on page 20 indicates that mine do have slight markings on the back of the head. Breeders who are aiming for perfect, all-white specimens can breed this out with careful selective breeding. Beak and legs are pinkish brown and eyes are dark brown.

Male and female are identical, although the female grows to a larger size, particularly noticeable once breeding starts.

Tuxedo: This is an apt name for a bird with a smart white waistcoat to contrast with its dark brown overcoat. The colour of the back feathers is identical with that of the American Range, indicating the close connection with that variety as well as with the English White.

The ideal markings are a clear white face, chest and belly, with brown back, tail and crown. In good specimens, the brown and white feathering is neatly demarcated, but it is common to find patches of white where the brown should be, and vice versa. If you look at the photograph on page 14, you will see that one of my Tuxedos has a white splash on the left side of his head, and has brown cheeks instead of white.

Commercial producers of eggs and table quail will tend to concentrate on the straight Coturnix laying strains bred by commercial breeders. On a smaller scale, there is no reason why the interested reader should not go in for the coloured variations of Coturnix. They are often prettier and are usually good egg producers. Egg production levels can, of course, be increased by selective breeding, and it is really the particular strain which is relevant in this respect. In addition to the normal Coturnix laying quail, I have American Range, English White, Fawn and Tuxedo. The first do lay more than the others but the difference is not that marked and would only be

The Bobwhite quail, a breed indigenous to the American continent.

unacceptable in a commercial egg production unit. On a small scale, many breeders find that concentrating on the coloured varieties is not only more interesting, but they are able to concentrate on selling breeding pairs or trios of stock, rather than on eggs.

Coturnix eggs

The eggs of Coturnix birds are off-white splashed with chocolate brown. The latter may be in the form of tiny spots, large spots or large splodges. There is a considerable variation in patterning.

I once tried to keep a record of all the variations of patterning, hoping that I would be able to identify particular eggs as belonging to specific hens, without having to trap nest. I soon gave up because just when I thought I was getting somewhere, a new variation would appear. They also occasionally produce olive-coloured eggs with no markings at all, just to be perverse. Occasionally, some strains will produce all-white eggs as a mutation.

The size is approximately one third that of a chicken's egg (see the photograph on page 56). In the wild, about a dozen eggs are laid in a clutch, with two or possibly three clutches in a season. Selectively bred strains can produce between 150-200 eggs without artificial light. The provision of light and good winter management can increase this to 200-300 eggs. It should be emphasized, however, that to achieve such production levels requires the use of good commercial strains, and a high level of management.

The Bobwhite quail

The **Bobwhite** quail, *Colinus virginianus*, is a breed which has its distribution mainly in North and Central America. Alternative names are **American** or **Partridge** quail. The latter name is an appropriate one for it is much more like a partridge than a quail.

There are over twenty sub-species, such as the **Masked Bobwhite**, *Colinus v. ridgwayi*, a breed currently on the endangered species list.

The breed most commonly kept in captivity is the **Common Bobwhite**, *Colinus virginianus*. In Britain, it is regarded as an aviary bird. In the USA it is a game bird in the wild, an aviary bird on a small scale and, on a larger scale, is often kept as a commercial egg producer or table bird.

The Bobwhite is a bigger bird altogether than the Coturnix layer, with the male reaching 9½'' and female 10½''. For this reason, it is regarded more as a meat bird than an egg producer by some, although commercial establishments in the USA normally have the two enterprises running together.

The back, tail and crown of both sexes is dark brown, while the chest, belly and flanks are lighter, with black and white striations. A white stripe covers the eyebrows and, in the male, there is a white patch under the chin. In some females, this patch is absent or reduced, being replaced by buff markings. The overall colour effect is less bright in the female. The beak is greyish-brown, legs yellowish-brown and eyes dark brown.

Chinese Painted quail, the smallest breed and a popular choice for the aviary.

The Bobwhite is a most attractive bird (see the photograph on page 22). I have a pair in the aviary and they have proved to be easy to tame as I have already mentioned.

They have a greater tendency to fly and perch than other breeds of quail, so they really need perching facilities.

They can sometimes prove to be aggressive with smaller breeds, but I have never found this to be so with mine which cohabit quite happily with Chinese Painted quail and some of the coloured varieties of Coturnix. I should emphasize however, that I keep relatively small numbers of each breed, and have succeeded in taming my breeding stock to the extent that they will come when called. Anyone keeping larger numbers, on a commercial basis, would obviously keep them separate; and would have less time for regular conversations with their birds.

Bobwhite eggs

The eggs are slightly bigger than those of Coturnix breeds, and generally have a paler appearance. The background colour is off-white with a fine speckling of brown spots. There is a variation in patterning, with some eggs having bolder markings than others, but on the

24

whole, they are more finely marked.

In the wild, up to about two dozen eggs are produced in a season. Selectively-bred specimens in protected conditions can produce 50-100 eggs a year, with no extra light. With the provision of artificial light, the provision of winter quarters and adequate feed rations, this can be increased to 150-200 a year.

Chinese Painted quail

The **Chinese Painted quail**, *Excalfactoria chinensis*, is probably the most widely kept of the ornamental aviary breeds. It is easily the prettiest and most colourful, and in recent years has been much utilized as a spider catcher in butterfly houses. Anyone who has ever visited one of the increasing number of butterfly breeding establishments, such as that at Syon Park in Middlesex, will have seen these busy little birds scuttling through the ground vegetation of the greenhouses, beady eyes on the lookout for unwary spiders and ground insects.

Found in China, India, Sri -Lanka, South Africa and Australia, the Chinese Painted quail is also known as the **King** quail and the **Blue breasted** quail, and there are several sub-species.

It is the smallest of all the quail breeds, with the male reaching 4½" and the female 5". The male is much more colourful than the female, with brown and black flecked back and crown, bluish-grey breast and face, reddish-brown belly and tail feathers and black and white striped chin and throat. The female is mainly a dullish-brown with black and white flecks. She has a white patch on the throat, but the black bars on the throat and face are absent. The beak is black in both sexes, eyes brown

There are variations to these basic standards, with a white, silvery-white and fawnish-brown type. The various sub-species also show differences. The **African Blue-breasted** quail, *Excalfactoria adansonii*, has the male much darker backed, but with the wings striped chestnut brown and grey. The **Australian King** quail, *E. chinensis lineata*, has more strongly marked lines, as the Latin name implies.

Chinese Painted quail eggs

The eggs are considerably smaller than those of the Coturnix quail (see the photograph on page 56 for a visual comparison). They are a dull bluish-grey in colour. In the wild, about a dozen eggs are produced in a season. In aviary bred and managed birds, this number will be increased to around 50, and the provision of artificial light will further increase the total. However, it is not usual to give Chinese Painted quail artificial light, as is the case with the Coturnix breeds, unless it is to produce early eggs for incubation.

The question is often asked: Can one eat the eggs? There is no reason why they should not be eaten, but they are much smaller than Coturnix eggs, and it seems hardly worth it. There is also the aspect that there is a ready market for Chinese Painted quail within the pet and aviary market, so it is much more profitable to incubate the eggs and sell the young through local pet shops.

Ornamental species of quail

Although the Chinese Painted quail and the coloured varieties of Coturnix are often regarded as ornamentals, and frequently kept in aviaries as such, there is also a growing interest in the rarer, more exotic breeds. Two popular choices, in this respect, are the California quail, *Callipepla Californica (Lophortyx Californica)* and the Mountain quail, *Oreortyx picta*, illustrated opposite. Both these breeds are notable for the head plumage. That of the Mountain quail sweeps back in a straight line while that of the smaller California quail curves forwards. They adapt well to aviary conditions, but must have winter protection, and need separate accommodation for breeding purposes.

Other exotic breeds which are bred in captivity in the UK include Gambel's quail, *Callipepla gambelii*, Scaled quail, *Callipepla squamata*, Elegant quail, *Callipepla douglasii*, Harlequin quail, *Coturnix delegorguei*, Rain quail, *Coturnix coromandelica*, Masked Bobwhite, *Colinus v. ridgwayi*, and Crested Bobwhite, *Colinus cristatus*. Some of these are available only in limited numbers

California quail

Mountain quail

and the price of rarer species can be as high as £150-£200 a pair. There is also the question of responsibility in relation to rarer species, that no-one should consider taking them on without having regard for the need to maintain or increase numbers by careful breeding. Reference has already been made to the fact that the Masked Bobwhite is currently on the endangered species list, and strenuous efforts are being made to increase its numbers in the wild. Anyone interested in this aspect should contact the Quail Group of The World Pheasant Association which is active in this context. One of the main breeders of ornamental quail in the UK is Michael Summerlin, but as I mentioned earlier, some species are available only in limited numbers. Appropriate addresses are to be found in the Reference section.

Commercial strains of Coturnix laying quail housed in battery cages in protected housing. Photo by courtesy of Poultry World.

Housing

The system of housing depends very much on the type and scale of the quail enterprise. A commercial system will be more intensive than that where birds are kept primarily for interest. The more exotic breeds will usually be in aviaries, either indoor or outdoor, with attached house. A small-scale enterprise may utilise small houses and runs. Whichever system is used, the salient point is that quail are not winter hardy and will need adequate winter housing.

Most commercial enterprises will use either a cage system or a floor-rearing one. The former is where purpose-made cages, equipped with automatic watering facilities are used. The latter is where a building with a concrete floor is furnished with wood shavings, feeders and drinkers, and the birds can roam at will within the confines of the house.

A concrete floor is essential, and the building needs to be substantial enough, not only to deter rodents but also to provide draught-free and well-ventilated, sheltered accommodation.

Ventilation by roof ridge and side window is ideal, as a through current of fresh air is provided. The arrangement of this will vary depending on the type of house. Very large houses will use fans.

Lighting in a house is not only necessary for efficient management, but it will also provide a stimulus for winter eggs. Further information on this is given on page 68.

Heating in winter is not necessary as long as there is adequate insulation. This can be in the form of insulation boards purchased from a DIY centre and hammered onto the inside roof and walls. Alternatively, a relatively new technique is to spray insulation on the walls and roof. Newly-hatched quail will naturally have localised heat in the form of brooder lamps until they are hardy.

29

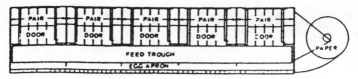

5 cage Sani-Battery unit for 5 pairs of quail

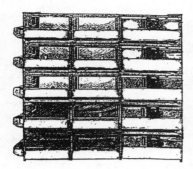

Above: American battery unit available from Marsh Farms (USA). Droppings fall through and are caught on the paper which goes underneath the cages. To provide new lining is simply a matter of pulling on the roll from the left side. Illustration by courtesy of Marsh Farms.

Left: Stacked cage units available from Curfew (UK).

(See also Appendix 1 on page 87)

Cage systems

Cages of the type supplied by Curfew, allow a substantial amount of room and can be stacked up to five sections, an overall height of 6'3''. Each unit has a drop-tray for ease of cleaning, and feeders and drinkers are provided at the ends and sides of the cages. Automatic watering in the form of header tank, pipes and clips can provide a round-the-clock supply of fresh water.

These particular cages can be used in association with Curfew tiered brooders. Quail chicks can then be raised from day-olds in the brooders until they are three weeks old when the brooders are switched off. The brooder area and run can then be used for the main runs.

It is possible to make your own cages, of course, and welded mesh is the most suitable material. A protective strip for the edges of cut welded mesh is available by the metre, from cage suppliers such as Curfew.

Some people prefer to make their own cages using a wooden framework. Other alternatives are to adapt rabbit hutches or wooden bird breeding cages.

Alternatives to the battery cage

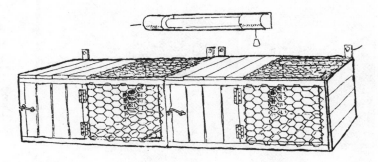

A system of indoor rabbit hutches adapted by the author to provide quail housing. The covered areas provide sleeping accommodation while the wire mesh on the roof of the living area allows adequate light to enter to ensure winter egg production.

There are many people, myself included, who dislike the battery cage system, particularly when the cages are overstocked. The use of wire bottoms for the cages facilitates cleaning and prevents a possible build-up of disease, but does mean that the birds are unable to scratch in the way they do in unrestricted conditions. For this reason, some quail breeders prefer to use wooden bird breeding cages, with solid wooden floors, sides and roofs, and a mesh cage front. These require a greater degree of management, because the wood shavings floor litter does need to be cleared out regularly. However, these wooden cages are usually equipped with a sliding floor section so that cleaning is not that great a task.

An idea which may be of interest to those who favour a less intensive approach is the system of adapting rabbit hutches which I evolved some years ago. The details are shown in the diagram above. The floor on one side of the hutch was removed and replaced by wire mesh of the sort normally used for cage floors. The section of roof above was also removed and treated in the same way so that, in winter, extra light was made available for out of season laying. A bank of these in an outhouse, worked well.

Young quail being raised on a floor system in protected housing. Photo by courtesy of Poultry World.

Floor systems

A floor-system is inside a building where the door has an interior flight entrance. This is essentially to stop birds escaping when you open the door, and works on the 'air-lock' principle. In other words, you close the outside door before opening the interior one. It need not necessarily be a door; it could be strips of wood or wire mesh strategically placed to provide a barrier.

Concrete floors really are essential for such a system, for rats are highly intelligent and devious in their efforts to gain entry into an area where there are vulnerable young birds.

Wood shavings provide the best litter material. They are clean, absorbent and also absorb smells. Suspended feeders and drinkers are probably best in this sort of situation, for they are less likely to have litter scratched into them.

A less intensive floor-system for those who like to give their birds more freedom, is one which has the inside run extending outside. An example is shown in the illustration on page 35. Here, the birds range on the concrete floor with wood shavings inside the house and also on a concrete run outside, via a pop-hole. Again, concrete is a good idea here, not only because the run is rat-proof, but droppings can be swept with a broom, and if necessary, hosed down when the birds are confined inside by closing the pop-hole. Naturally, woodshavings are not used in the outside run.

The outside run is enclosed by stout wire mesh of a gauge too fine to allow rodents to enter and the bottom section has protective boards which help to protect against the wind. It is about 3' high with a gate for human access, making run clearance easier.

The provision of a certain amount of natural cover will be welcomed by the birds. Terry Rolph, the breeder of Crusader Coturnix quail, tells me that some conifer branches placed in one corner are suitable, or conifer trees in pots. Bracken cuttings and various logs have also been used to good effect. Even if the run is completely contained within a building, the provision of such cover is appreciated.

A series of interlocking posts and game netting can be used to make internal pens in a building where a floor system is in use. This simplifies management and prevents mass panic when the birds crowd in the same direction at the same time. It can also be used to make internal divisions in an aviary, as well as temporary outside pens in the summer. Another application is as an internal door in a floor system building, preventing birds escaping when the main door is opened. Photos by courtesy of Agriframes Ltd.

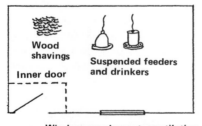

Wood shavings

Suspended feeders and drinkers

Inner door

Window supplements ventilation

Two ways of using a building for a floor system of rearing

For egg production, the provision of artificial light to supply a total of 16 hours of natural/artificial light is necessary.

For table birds, no artificial light should be given otherwise growth is slowed down.

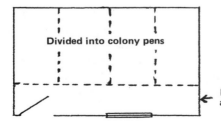

Divided into colony pens

← Inner passage for access and food storage area

A less intensive floor system, where the quail have access to an outside concrete run via a 'pop-hole'.

Aviary systems

Quail breeders of rarer species of quail often use aviary systems of one sort or another. The simplest of these is the small house with attached run, or a bank of these arranged in such a way that the individual runs are parallel with each other, but separate, so that different breeds are kept apart. It is normal for specific breeds to be kept in pairs, but several pairs should not be kept together because the males may fight. Hen birds of the same variety can normally be housed together.

Many breeders, particularly of the more ornamental varieties, like to have runs with natural vegetation. It is possible to arrange this, as long as precautions to deter rats are taken. I have already referred to the fact that concrete runs are the safest, but strong wire mesh laid on the ground and extending beyond the perimeter is a good alternative. Once in position, rubble is placed on top, followed by soil and a layer of sand. Small shrubs or other plants can then be planted directly into the soil. Long grasses are particularly suitable for they emulate the conditions which many breeds of quail frequent in the wild. As long as there is a quiet, protected corner with such plants, many quail breeds will build nests and incubate their eggs. The Chinese Painted quail, for example, will make a nest in the middle of a clump of long grass, while Coturnix breeds will also become broody, particularly in their second year.

35

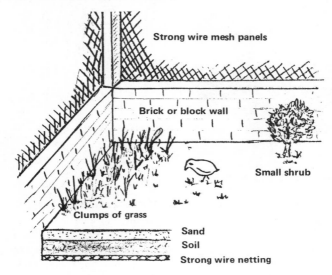

An outside run for hardier breeds of quail. A house inside the run, or attached to it, will still be necessary.

Strong wire mesh panels

Brick or block wall

Small shrub

Clumps of grass

Sand
Soil
Strong wire netting

It is necessary to sound a note of warning about the type of netting used underneath the soil in runs such as this. I once used netting which was slightly rusty. I reasoned that it was not good enough for anything else but was quite suitable for putting under the soil. It was a grave error! Rats discovered a weak point and burrowed under the perimeter wall, coming straight up in the centre of the run. They killed the three Japanese quail, one male and two females, who were residents.

A really rat-proof floor is provided by using flag stones instead of netting. These placed close together will exclude even the most devious of rats, while the cracks between them will provide necessary drainage. Rubble, soil and finally sand can then be placed on top as before.

Sand is recommended because it does allow the birds to make their own dust-bathing depressions, as well as providing a popular scratching area. Some breeders recommend this also as a means of deterring earthworms from coming to the surface. Earthworms are hosts to a number of parasites which can be transmitted to quail.

The author's male and female Japanese strain of Coturnix laying quail in an outside concrete run which has an attached house.

An outside aviary run of this type also needs protective walls at the base, with wire mesh above. The ideal, particularly for smaller quail such as the Chinese Painted which can escape through small crevices, is a solid wall five to six horizontal brick level high. This also provides wind and draught protection.

Within such an aviary, any stout house which is rain and draught-proof is suitable. In milder areas of the country, hardier breeds of quail can be left in outdoor runs, as long as their houses are well insulated. In more exposed areas, many breeders transfer their breeding stock to breeding cages inside a shed or aviary house, moving them out again in spring. This practice allows time for a good winter clean up of the outdoor aviaries, as well as a time for doing any necessary repairs. It is good practice, at this time, to sprinkle some lime on the empty run — just enough to give the impression of a light dusting of snow. It helps to clear the ground of any residual pests which may cause disease. The ground itself also has time to recover before the birds are returned to their summer quarters. Some breeders remove the top few inches of soil and replace it with fresh soil.

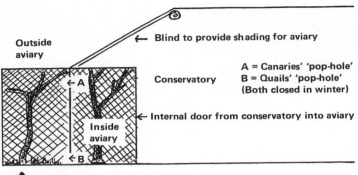

Outside aviary

← Blind to provide shading for aviary

Conservatory

A = Canaries' 'pop-hole'
B = Quails' 'pop-hole'
(Both closed in winter)

← A

← Internal door from conservatory into aviary

Inside aviary

← B

↑ External door into outside aviary

A small aviary built onto a conservatory, allowing winter and summer accommodation.

One of the nicest aviary systems I saw was where a quail breeder had built it half in and half out of her conservatory. During the spring, summer and autumn, the quail, which in this case were Chinese Painted, were able to move from the inside aviary to the outside one by means of a sliding door partition at the base. The aviary was a tall one which also housed canaries. They too had a sliding door partition, higher up on the dividing wall, and had access to the outside run when conditions were suitable.

Chinese Painted quail are frequently kept in avaiaries where tree perching birds are kept because they help to clear up the seeds spilt by the flying birds. This should not be regarded as the sole source of food for them however. It is not enough for they need a properly balanced diet like any other species. (See the section on Feeding.) In this context, I should mention a lady who kept Java finches, her prime interest. She had introduced several Chinese Painted quail into the bottom of the aviary because someone had told her they were useful to clean up aviary floors. She telephoned me to say that they 'kept dying' and did I know why? During the course of the conversation it emerged that not only did they have no food other than what the finches spilt, but had no house or any form of shelter other than the sapling which was planted in the aviary. Yet the Java finches had a proper diet and sheltered accommodation.

Some of the author's quail in a small movable run on grass. This is temporary accommodation, giving them access to grass during warm summer days. They are normally housed in a house with attached concrete run in the summer, and are moved into bird cages inside for the winter.

      Chinese Painted quail are ground-orientated birds and need to have proper rations and clean water provided for them in suitable containers on the ground, rather than having to rely on the occasional spilt seeds falling like manna from above. They also need proper housing which will provide warmth and shelter, free of damp and draughts. A fairly simple house is all that is necessary, but it should have woodshavings or other warm nesting material to provide insulation. Brookside Aviaries manufacture such quail houses for up to six birds. They are intended for use in aviaries not for outside use.

Two aviaries suitable for quail
on the ground and flying birds
such as canaries or finches above.
The one on the left is an outside aviary with winter housing
behind, while the one on the right is an inside one suitable
for a conservatory or other building. Photos by courtesy of
Southern Aviaries.

A poultry broody box
and run suitable as a
quail house and run
for a breeding pair
or trio, or for young
quail in the warm
weather.

**DESIGN FOR A SMALL
QUAIL HOUSE AND RUN**

Roof overhangs part of
run to give added rain
and wind protection.

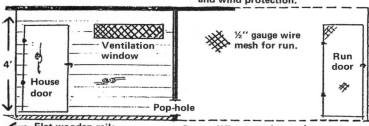

½'' gauge wire
mesh for run.

Ventilation
window

Run
door

4'

House
door

Pop-hole

← Flat wooden rails
allowing house to
be pulled easily to
a new site.

Strong ½'' gauge wire mesh
for rat-proof floor to run,
but allows grass to get through

If insulation of house is adequate, laying
quail can overwinter here, but they need
artificial light not only to produce winter
eggs, but to keep active for longer periods,
thus generating warmth.

Internal netting can be erected to
prevent head banging on the roof

40

The movable house and run

If small numbers of quail are to be kept outside an aviary or house, the best solution is to use a strong house and run of the type used by poultrykeepers for hens and chicks. These can be moved from one area of grass to another, allowing them access to clean pasture on a regular basis. The house needs a well boarded floor capable of deterring rats, so that once shut up for the night the birds are safe from harm. The run which has a wire floor resting on the grass, is obviously safer than the floorless type.

With such a system, it is a good idea to keep specific breeds together, rather than mix them up, although females of the various Coturnix varieties will cohabit successfully. Males housed together may fight and should, as a rule, be kept separate from each other. One male can usually accompany up to around half a dozen females, although it is worth remembering that Chinese Painted quail are monogamous and normally kept in pairs.

It is advisable to remember that quail are not naturally hardy birds. While a small house and run may be satisfactory in the warmer months, it is not usually successful in winter. My own practice is to have the birds in a house and run in summer and then to transfer them to indoor breeding cages for the winter. Incidentally, I find it safer to put the runs on a concrete area rather than on grass, not only because they are safer from predators, but also to minimise the risk of infection from droppings. All that is necessary is to confine them to the house, sweep out the concrete run then hose it down. They have a box of sand in which to make dust baths, and some branches placed to provide shade and slightly more natural conditions.

It is possible, in milder areas of the country, to have quail in outdoor houses and runs in winter, but even in such areas of Britain, recent winters have been severe, and I would advise against it. Having said that, I have heard of a lady in Sussex who has a few quail completely free-ranging in her back garden all through the year. So far, she has been lucky.

Coturnix quail are at risk from damaging their heads by flying straight up and banging themselves in low-roofed houses or runs.

I must mention again the tendency of Coturnix quail to fly up in the air and bang their heads on the roof of the run. It has been claimed by numerous authorities that they only do this in the breeding season, but in my experience, this is quite untrue. They will fly up and crack their heads at any time of year. It is also untrue that if there is a solid roof, rather than a wire mesh one, they will not bang themselves. They do! The best way to deal with this is to attach some plastic or fine string netting about a foot below the roof so that they do not injure themselves. This was a tip which I originally had from Victoria Roberts of The Domestic Fowl Trust, and it works.

Fawn Coturnix quail in a movable run on grass.

Coping with the head bangers

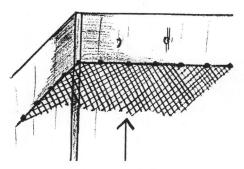

Plastic or string netting protects the birds from banging their heads on the roof.

Quail flies straight upwards

Feeding

Quail need a 27% protein ration and it is often difficult to find a ready formulated quail feed which provides this. Most large producers make up their own feeds, buying in the appropriate ingredients from their local mill. A favourite mixture is as follows:

6 parts Turkey crumbs : 1 part 18% Pheasant crumbs

Smaller units, particularly those operating on an aviary basis, make up their own rations using a wider variety of ingredients, and including grain. Such a formula might be:

1 part oatmeal : 1 part chick crumbs : 1 part millet : 1 part shelled canary seed.

There are aviary feed specialists which make this mixture available as a 'quail mixture'. Although the ingredients tend to be the same, the proportions in relation to each other may be different.

As far as my own quail are concerned, I make up a mixture as follows:

1 part chick crumbs : 1 part canary seed : 1 part millet

In addition to this, they have surplus lettuce leaves, and outer leaves from kitchen garden vegetables. They also have access to grit which is, of course, essential where grain is given, for the proper functioning of the crop in breaking down and digesting seeds. I should make it clear that while this feeding pattern is ideal for rearing healthy, lively quail on a small scale, it would not be practicable or realistic for a large unit.

It is worth mentioning that for the chicks of Chinese Painted quail even chick crumbs may prove to be too coarse for the first few days. My practice is to grind some up to make it finer for them, but it is only necessary to

One of the author's Coturnix laying quail housed in a bird breeding cage during the winter. In cold weather, the feed requirements are higher to cater for extra energy needed to keep warm.

do this for about a week.

Another point worth making is that some feed manufacturers now produce a 28% protein pheasant ration. I have not yet tried it, but it could well be suitable for quail, if the price is reasonable. It is worth enquiring at your local mill or feed supplier.

Perhaps one of the most unusual quail diets I have come across is that adopted by a contributor to 'Home Farm' magazine who lives in a New York apartment. He rears quail in a range of old fish tanks and also raises earthworms and catfish. He mixes his feed in a 30 gallon capacity bucket, using a trowel as a scoop, and his formula is as follows:

½ scoop alfalfa meal : 1 scoop mixed dried roots, seeds and leaves : 1 scoop chopped wheat sprouts : 1 tablespoon iodized salt : 1 tablespoon ground limestone.

This is supplemented with surplus baby catfish, live worms and freshly shredded greens. The New York diet certainly ensures that the quail have enough protein, but there would be few people dedicated enough to follow it.

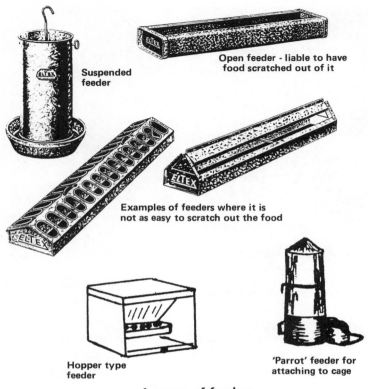

Suspended feeder

Open feeder - liable to have food scratched out of it

Examples of feeders where it is not as easy to scratch out the food

Hopper type feeder

'Parrot' feeder for attaching to cage

A range of feeders suitable for quail

Illustrations by courtesy of George H. Elt Ltd., and Southern Aviaries.

Feed equipment

Quail are inveterate scratchers and will propel their food in all directions if given the opportunity to do so. Those in commercial cage systems will probably have external feed troughs so that only the head can reach them. Where a floor system is used, suspended feeders which are clear of the ground are the most suitable. If they are gravity-fed or hopper type feeders, the surface area presented to the bird is small enough to prevent jumping up and scratching, yet gravity fills up the feeding area as the feed is eaten.

Automatic drinkers for use with a header tank

Suspended drinker   **Free-standing drinker**   **Clip-on drinker**   **'Parrot' drinker**

Some examples of drinkers suitable for quail

I have found that using flat open containers is a waste of time. The quail merely jump in and scratch the food everywhere. One might as well put it all on the floor in the first place. If the birds are in a concrete run, and the weather is dry, then adopting this latter course is suitable. A concrete run can be kept clean easily by sweeping and hosing down.

Commercially, feed is available at all times, with the birds helping themselves from the feed troughs on an ad-lib basis. Each adult quail will consume about 4½ oz a week. On a smaller scale, feeding twice a day is enough, as long as sufficient feed is given. With my rule-of-thumb approach, I find that one of my handfuls (I have small hands) is enough for six quail at a time, and I feed morning and afternoon. This is a fairly general estimate of course, and there are bound to be variations. Some birds naturally eat more than others, while temperature fluctuations will also have a bearing on consumption: they eat more in winter in order to keep warm.

Water

Clean water is essential at all times and there is no question of making this available a couple of times a day. It must be there whenever the birds feel like drinking, which could be anytime. Again, a commercial unit will normally have an automatic system which utilizes a header tank, tubing, connectors and the drinkers themselves. In a floor system, suspended drinkers as part of an automatic system work well.

On a smaller scale, suspended drinkers which operate on a gravity-principle are satisfactory. This is the type I use for my quail, and I find that refilling once a day is enough to ensure a supply of water for 24 hours. When my quail are brought inside to their wooden canary breeding cages for the winter, I use parrot drinkers. These clip onto the bars of the front of the cage and one of these is enough for a pair of birds for 24 hours. I should add that, in these circumstances, I have no choice but to use flat open dishes for their food, and have to put up with a certain amount of food scratching and dispersal.

Grit

Although a proprietary mixture such as the turkey crumb/pheasant crumb mixture, referred to on page 44, is said to be a balanced diet without the need of extra grit, I have my reservations about this. It has always been my experience that birds need a small amount of extra grit, and I prefer to err on the side of caution by making it available to them. If grains such as millet, or chopped wheat are given then grit is absolutely essential otherwise the crop which is responsible for grinding up the grain particles cannot function properly.

On a commercial scale, where feed may be made available on a conveyor system, the grit can be incorporated into the feed at the mixing stage. On a smaller scale, the odd handful given separately on the ground about once a week is sufficient. Fine grit suitable for quail is available from most pet-shops or aviary suppliers. Branded supplies usually contain added minerals which help to keep the stock healthy. Grit supplied by poultry suppliers for chickens may prove to be too coarse for quail.

Special purpose diets

The commercial diet of turkey crumbs and pheasant crumbs is suitable for all ages of quail, although reference has already been made to the need to grind up feeds for the chicks of Chinese Painted quail. It can be used as a rearing feed, as a layers' ration for egg production and as a fattening feed for table quail production.

Some of the ornamental breeds kept in aviaries may need a certain amount of live food, particularly if they are to be persuaded to hatch and rear their own young. The most convenient is purchased mealworms from an angling shop or aviary suppliers. These will be in bran and in a clean condition where disease transference is avoided. But a word of warning here! Always cut them in half before feeding. Whole ones have been known to tunnel in the gut if swallowed whole, before the digestive juices have rendered them harmless.

Green food

I have already referred to the fact that my quail have kitchen garden surpluses such as overblown lettuce. They quickly shred their way through such leaves with their sharp beaks, and it is arguable that this activity has a beneficial effect in preventing feather pecking or other aggressive behaviour, rather than the strictly nutritional benefits. Most commercial quail would not have access to green food, although I draw your attention to the Appendix on page 87 which describes how at least one commercial producer regularly puts her birds out to grass. It is certainly my belief that quail are healthier, happier and longer-lived when they have a good basic diet with lots of variety. If it is true for humans, then why not for quail?

Breeding

Breeding is an essential aspect of keeping quail, whether on a large or a small scale. Large production units in the UK tend to breed and rear their own replacement breeding stock, rather than buy in 'point-of-lay' stock, as is the case in the poultry world. The reason for this is because the selective breeding of quail has not taken place to the same degree as it has with poultry. As I have already mentioned, there are some large breeders such as Curfew, Fayre Game and Marsh who selectively breed and sell commercial strains but it is still not a widespread practice. Most producers find that it is better to breed their own replacements, buying in new breeders for the breeding flock as and when necessary.

Smaller enterprises, which often have the coloured and ornamental breeds, generally find that breeding such stock has a ready market among interested poultry keepers, rare breed enthusiasts and aviary owners. Whatever the scale, breeding quail has a fascination which few could doubt. I find it the most interesting aspect of all.

Breeding stock

It goes without saying that the breeding stock should be healthy, have no visible defects and be unrelated. The latter consideration is often overlooked, and purchasers of a pair of a particular breed, may unknowingly have acquired a brother and sister. Such inbreeding can result in genetic defects being thrown up in the progeny. I once found that a clutch of Japanese Coturnix chicks had three born without claws on the feet. They were the progeny of a pair which I had bought specifically as breeders. What I should have done, of course, was to have acquired them from different sources, or bought two pairs, one from each source, and swapped over the males.

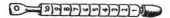 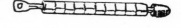

Above — Closed aluminium rings which are put on when the chicks are a few days old. Marked with the current year, they guarantee the age of the bird. Coturnix quail take size R while Chinese Painted quail take size L.

Ring open

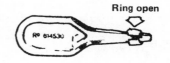

Right — Plastic split rings available in 12 single colours or 76 striped colours. They are used for the identification of breeding stock and breeding lines. They can be put on at any age with the aid of an opening tool, as shown. Coturnix quail take size 1FB while Chinese Painteds take size XB.

Illustrations by courtesy of Southern Aviaries.

The use of leg rings is essential in order to keep adequate records and to ensure that you know which bird is which. Normal poultry leg rings are too large, but quail rings are available from specialist suppliers, listed in the reference section. These can be obtained in different colours, and in a numbered sequence if required. They are available in plastic or aluminium.

Before collecting eggs for incubation, the male and females should have been confined together in breeding quarters for at least a week, and it is as well to discard the eggs for incubating for the first few days afterwards (although they should still be collected) until they have settled down into a regular output. Coturnix quail can be kept in pairs, trios or one male for 5 - 6 females. Bobwhites are normally kept in pairs, although there is no reason why the number of females should not be increased. Chinese Painted quail are naturally monogamous and should be kept in pairs. The rarer, ornamental breeds are usually kept in pairs or trios. If you want to keep a precise record of which hen is producing which egg, then the obvious solution is to house only a pair in the breeding quarters. Selective breeding for a particular characteristic is made much easier in this way. Selective breeding may be for a number of reasons: colour, feather markings, egg production, quick growth, weight — and so on. The basic principle which operates is that if you breed from two birds which both have a similar characteristic, their progeny will tend to have the same feature.

THE ESSENTIALS OF INCUBATION

TEMPERATURE — 37.7°C (100°F) in centre of egg
HUMIDITY — 65%. Increase to 70% 2 days before hatch
TURNING — 5 times a day

Good, healthy and
unrelated breeding
stock with proven
performance

Store fertile eggs at 14.5°C
with blunt end up, and at
angle of 45°. Reverse the
direction of tilt twice daily.
Incubate before 7 days old.

Incubate at temperature of 39.4°C
(103°F) when the thermometer is
2″ above the centre of the eggs in
a still air thermometer. The temperature in the middle of the egg should
not exceed 37.7°C (100°F).
Follow the manufacturer's instructions!

The humidity should be 65% for most
of the incubation period, increasing to
70% for the last 2 days before hatching.

If incubator does not have an
automatic turning facility, turn
the eggs five times a day. Wash
your hands before handling them.

After hatching, wait until the chicks
are dry and fluffed up before moving
to protected brooding conditions with
food and water.

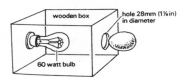

wooden box   hole 28mm (1⅛ in) in diameter

60 watt bulb

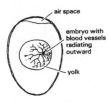

air space

embryo with
blood vessels
radiating
outward

yolk

Candle after 6-7 days if you must
to see which eggs are fertile and
which are not developing.

INCUBATION TIMES

Coturnix breeds	18 days
Bobwhite breeds	23 days
Chinese Painted	16 days

(These are average times - they may
vary by a couple of days each way)

Female Japanese Coturnix showing denuding of the head feathers during the breeding season.

In many commercial units, it is normal to have one male to each four hens in the cages and mixed running is no problem as far as commercial egg sales are concerned. The eggs are collected every morning and graded. The large and the small ones are selected for selling, while the medium-sized ones are retained for incubation. Of those hatched, most will be reared as table birds, while some are retained as future breeders. Stock birds which are eventually selected from these are then housed in trios in separate breeding accommodation. This pattern of operations is not standard, of course, and there will be many variations, depending on the unit concerned.

Coturnix quail will start to lay at around five weeks old, and the eggs will be fertile from about 6 weeks onwards. The behaviour of the male will leave no doubt as to when the fertile stage is reached because he will produce 'foam balls' and deposit them on the ground. The photographs on page 54 illustrate this. Once the male is sexually active, he will mate frequently with the females, gripping the feathers on the top of their heads with his beak. The photograph above shows how a certain amount of feather denuding of the head occurs at

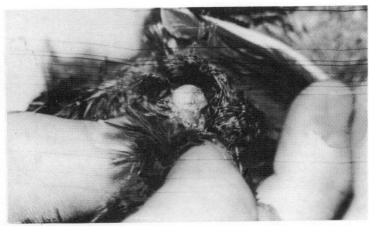

Above: The foam ball of the male bird. Photo:Mark Bomer
Left: Foam ball deposited on the ground. Compare the size with a pound coin.

this time. Occasionally, the skin is pierced leaving a wound. If this happens, the female should be removed immediately, in case the bloodstain incites aggressive attack. A period in a hospital cage in solitary confinement will soon enable her to recover. Occasionally, a male will object to a particular female for no apparent reason, attacking her in a vicious way. When this happens, there is no other solution but to split them up permanently.

Storing eggs prior to incubation

Once the eggs have been selected for incubation, they should be incubated as soon as possible, and certainly no later than a week after being laid. They need to be stored in a cool room at around 15°C (the optimum is 14.5°C), with the pointed end down. The photograph on page 57 shows this operation in progress in the hatchery of a large commercial quail farm. The eggs are turned through 45° morning and evening, until they are placed in the incubator. On a small scale they can be placed in cartons, such as that illustrated on page 65, with one end balanced on a brick, while a second brick stops it slipping. The carton is tipped in the other direction, at 45°C, with the change taking place twice a day.

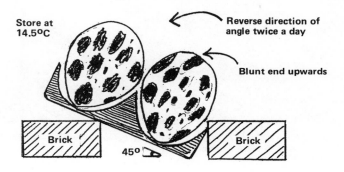

On a large scale, commercial hatcheries will fumigate or otherwise disinfect their hatching eggs to ensure that they are disease-free. On a small scale this is probably unnecessary but it is still important to wash your hands before handling them and to remember to do so before you turn them in the incubator, if you need to do so manually.

Natural incubation

Coturnix quail are not particularly good mothers in captivity, although they will become broody and sit on their own eggs if conditions are acceptable to them. They are more likely to do this in a floor-system or in an aviary, where a certain amount of natural cover and vegetation is present. They can cover about ten eggs at a time. Bantam hens such as Silkies or Silkie crosses have been used with success to hatch quail, but I have never tried this. I would be interested to hear from anyone who has.

Left to right: A chicken's egg, a Coturnix quail egg and a Chinese Painted quail egg. (The photograph is half normal size.)

Artificial incubation

Most quail are incubated artificially and certainly on a commercial scale, it is essential. Large units will have a separate setting room and incubation room. On a smaller scale, most general purpose small incubators are satisfactory for quail. I have used a Bristol incubator for a number of years and have had good results for quail, poultry and waterfowl with it. Of course, the eggs have to be turned manually and this is a nuisance when it needs to be done three times, and ideally five times, a day. A quail breeder in the West Country told me that he had consistently poor hatchings with a manually operated incubator, and when he went over to using an incubator with automatic turning facilities, his problems ceased. Certainly, the new small electronic incubator with such a facility is an enormous step forward for the small poultry breeder. The one illustrated on page 58, for example, has egg dividers of varying sizes to cater for a range of different eggs. The ones in the photograph are specifically for quail eggs.

Quail eggs being set for storage prior to incubation, at a commercial hatchery. Photo by courtesy of Poultry World.

Regular turning is, of course, essential, if the developing embryo is not to stick to one side of the shell membranes with a resulting malformation. Automatic turning frees one from the chore of having to remember to do it at regular intervals (and how many of us are scrupulous in this?)

It is possible to candle the eggs at around 5 days, in order to discover which eggs are fertile and developing and which are not. Commercially this is done, so that efficient use of incubator space is maximised. On a small scale, it is hardly necessary, for incubation time is not that long: 18 days for Coturnix breeds, 16 for Chinese Painted quail and 23 days for Bobwhites. Anyway, I have always found that the speckled nature of quail eggs makes them quite difficult to candle effectively.

As far as effective overall incubation is concerned, the single most important piece of advice is to follow the individual manufacturer's advice to the letter. He knows his incubator better than anyone else, and will normally give good instructions for different breeds. The subject of

A small incubator with automatic turning facilities and adapted for quail eggs. Photo by courtesy of Brinsea Incubators.

incubation is covered in considerable depth in my book Incubation: A Guide to Hatching and Rearing. Details are available from Broad Leys Publishing (See References).

Brooding

It is often claimed that your problems with quail only start once they are hatched. Their small size certainly makes them more effective escapees than poultry chicks. A glance at the photograph on page 60 indicates the size of a newly hatched Coturnix quail. That of the Chinese Painted quail is around the size of a bumble bee. Any brooder housing will require finely meshed wire to ensure that they do not escape through the holes. I find that for Chinese Painted quail, an old fish tank with netting across the top is the safest brooder. It is illustrated on page 62. For Coturnix chicks I adapted an indoor rabbit hutch as shown on the same page, to provide heating from an infra-red bulb. This is confined to what had been the rabbit's sleeping accommodation and the presence of wood shavings as litter provides a warm, comfortable area. Food and water is made avail-

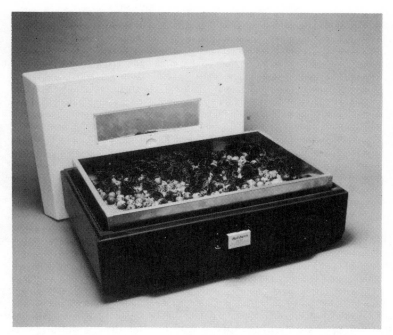

Newly hatched quail in a small incubator. Photo by courtesy of Brinsea Incubators.

able in the living accommodation half. I had to replace the existing bars of this section with fine wire mesh. That produced by Twilweld and available from many large garden centres or aviary suppliers is ideal. There are, of course, many possibilities when it comes to making home-made brooders and even a large cardboard box can be turned into an effective brooder.

Commercial brooding units are also available and, on a large scale, a floor system such as that shown on page 32 is ideal. Here, the quail chicks are on wood shavings in a rat-proof building with heat provided by overhead brooding units. Food is made available in shallow containers or chick feeders which allow the head to enter, but prevent them getting in to scratch out the food. Small, gravity-fed drinkers are available and the brooding area is confined to the vicinity of the lamps by wire netting lined with plastic feed sacks as insulation. As the chicks grow and develop, these confining walls are re-

A newly-hatched Coturnix quail chick.

moved and the artificial heat switched off. As a general rule, heat will be necessary for about three weeks, gradually raising the lamps to harden off the young birds. The outside temperature naturally has an influence, and in particularly cold periods, it may be necessary to extend the period of heating. Similarly, if it is warm, the availability of artificial heat can be reduced or withdrawn earlier.

Table quail will be ready for killing from the age of 6 weeks onwards when they have reached a liveweight of 6-7 oz.

Sexing quail

Coturnix laying quail are easy to sex because from about three weeks onwards, the reddish brown chest of the male will start to become noticeable. His markings are also more distinct and sharp than those of the female. Once they are adult and in breeding condition, from about 6 weeks onwards, the larger size of the female and the sexual behaviour and foam ball production of the male, referred to earlier, will be apparent. Before the age of 3 weeks, it is virtually impossible to sex the birds, and it is debatable whether it is necessary at this stage anyway.

The same chick, three days later.

The coloured varieties of Coturnix, such as English White, American Range and Tuxedo do not have an apparent difference in feathering between the male and female. The only way to tell them apart is to go by size difference — the female is bigger —, by sexual behaviour patterns and by vent examination. In the male this is more domed, while that of the female is more inverted, as shown in the illustration. This difference is only apparent after they have reached sexual maturity, when their behaviour will indicate their sexes anyway.

Also, in adulthood, is the difference in vocal sounds which have been mentioned earlier in the book.

Problems with young quail

Reference has already been made to the fact that young quail are escapees and that all cracks and crevices must be filled. The gauge of any netting used needs to be no bigger than ½", and that manufactured by Twilweld is ideal in this respect.

Their tendency to drown easily in shallow water should also be taken seriously, and for the first week,

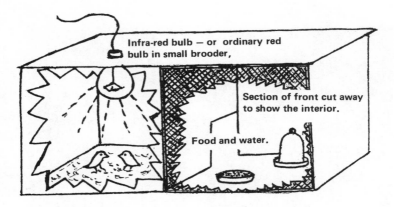

Infra-red bulb — or ordinary red bulb in small brooder,

Section of front cut away to show the interior.

Food and water.

A home-made brooder for a small number of young quail. It could be an adapted rabbit hutch or a large cardboard box.

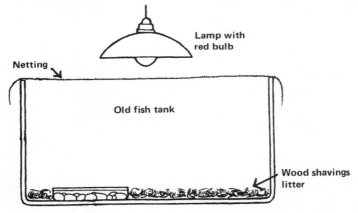

Lamp with red bulb

Netting

Old fish tank

Wood shavings litter

Some ideas on brooding young quail. (See page 32 for larger scale or commercial floor system).

Dull—emitter heater suitable for brooding young quail. Illustration by courtesy of George H. Elt Ltd.

Any water container should have pebbles placed in the water to make the depth shallower and prevent drowning.

drinkers need to have clean pebbles or marbles placed in them, so that the depth of water is reduced to a safe level, while still providing water for them to drink.

I have also referred to the effects of inbreeding of parent stock leading to genetic defects, such as my experience of having quail chicks born without claws. Another problem with feet which I discovered to my cost some years ago was when I used a brooder with under-floor heating. Although equipped with thermostat and having adequate insulation as well as wood shavings litter on top, the whole batch of quail developed the same foot problem. Basically this was a blackening of the toes, followed by rapid withering and ultimately the complete loss of them. (See the photograph on page 81). The whole batch had to be put down and I have never used this form of brooding again. The problem has never occurred since.

Egg production

In Britain, the same Coturnix quail are generally used for egg production as well as for the table trade. Although there has not been widespread selective breeding and development for commercial purposes, as with poultry, it has occurred on a limited basis.

Terry Rolph of Curfew, has developed his own 'Crusader' commercial strain, while in the USA, Marsh Farms have bred the 'Marsh Pharoah' strains for both eggs and table birds. In Japan, where selective breeding has perhaps been more intensive than anywhere else, various strains of Japanese quail have been developed for eggs, table birds and for laboratory research. In the USA, the Bobwhite quail is currently used for egg production to a limited degree, and also for table bird production.

Good commercial strains are therefore available and anyone thinking of starting a quail enterprise, is advised to invest in such stock. Once the enterprise is running smoothly you should also concentrate on doing your own selective breeding, by maintaining a breeding flock from which future quality birds can be selected. More information on this aspect is given in the section on 'Breeding'.

If the enterprise is to be a reasonably large one, sufficient to provide an adequate income, then it is difficult to see how anything other than a cage system or confined floor system, could be viable. The former is the most efficient in terms of management, as the eggs are easily collected. With a floor system, egg collection is more time-consuming and hazardous. Eggs tend to be laid anywhere and quail do not have a well-developed nest-laying instinct as do chickens. I have frequently stepped on eggs laid on the floor. They are small and the speckled nature of the shell has a camouflaging effect against the floor litter. In Britain, most quail eggs are produced in cage systems while table birds are produced in floor systems similar to that used for broiler chickens.

Purpose-made cartons are available for quail eggs and facilitate the marketing of fresh eggs.

Eggs should be collected at regular intervals on a daily basis and stored in a cool room at around 15°C. If any are to be incubated, it is best to select medium-sized ones for this purpose, leaving the larger and smaller ones for sale. At present, there is no system of grading the eggs, as is the case with chickens' eggs offered for sale.

With a cage system, it is highly unlikely that there will be any problem of soiling of eggs. If there are any lightly soiled eggs it is best to brush them with a clean, dry nailbrush. Heavily soiled ones can be washed in warm water with a purpose-made egg sanitising solution, but it is best to avoid selling soiled eggs. If they are cleaned with a sanitising solution, they are suitable for incubation purposes. In fact, many commercial breeders fumigate or otherwise clean and disinfect hatching eggs as a matter of course, in order to avoid egg infection.

Packing and selling eggs

Eggs are sold in several ways. The fresh eggs frequently go to hotels, quality restaurants, delicatessens, farm-gate shops or other retail outlets. At time of writing, my local delicatessen is selling fresh quail eggs at 14p each, a retail price of £1.68 per dozen.

Plastic egg cartons specifically for quail eggs are available from specialist suppliers. Packaging is an important aspect of marketing and the customer is far more likely to purchase eggs in an attractive package which will also protect the eggs during transit than in a loose paper bag. If the quantity of cartons purchased is large enough, it is usually possible to have descriptive labels with details of your own farm incorporated. Alternatively, it is possible to order labels that you can stick on yourself. There are printers who specialise in this form of label printing.

Eggs in brine

A more common form of egg marketing is to hard boil the eggs and put them in brine in a glass jar. The example shown in the photograph has six eggs in a jar with a metal crimped-on lid. This particular example is a product imported into the UK from France, and retailing at £1.20. In view of the potential for producing a home-grown product capable of competing favourably with imported examples, it makes one wonder why it is that British producers are apparently slow in facing up to the French challenge. I suspect that it is not the lack of enthusiasm on the part of producers, but the inability of distributors to accept new sources of supplies when they are already dealing with established producers such as the French.

Miniature Scotch eggs

A most enterprising British quail egg producer has evolved a novel way of giving his eggs value-added appeal. He hardboils them, removes the shells, coats them in flour and sausagemeat, with a final coating of breadcrumbs. Once deep-fried for a few moments, they

Quail eggs boiled and preserved in brine, sold as a quality delicatessen product.

provide miniature Scotch eggs, a delicacy which has obvious appeal for the delicatessen market.

Pickled eggs

In the USA, there is a considerable market for pickled quail eggs. These are hardboiled eggs which are then placed in commercial grade and distilled white vinegar for about twelve hours. This process dissolves the shells, when they are washed and refrigerated for a few hours. The eggs are then immersed in clean water while the membranes are removed by hand. At this stage, they are ready for immersion in the pickling solution. The one used by Marsh Farm in the USA is 1½ quarts water, 2½ quarts white vinegar, 1 cup of salt per gallon of liquid and 1 large chopped onion. A French producer I spoke to uses a similar pickling solution, but boils the vinegar with pickling spices first. This is then strained and cooled before being added to the other ingredients.

In Britain, fewer people produce pickled quail eggs, mainly because of the time and effort required in shell removal. There is also the undoubted visual appeal of the speckled shells which is lost with this process.

Quail eggs in aspic

Quail eggs in aspic is, of course, a well-known delicacy and another way of achieving the maximum return on the eggs. The eggs are hardboiled, then shelled. It is not necessary to dissolve them in vinegar as detailed above. They can be cracked, placed in cold water and have the shells and membranes removed simultaneously. For this, it is important not to use eggs that are too fresh for the shells are difficult to remove. Once they are several days old, the shells come off far more easily. If cut in half and placed in a small glass or plastic container with the yolk facing upwards, the aspic mixture can then be poured on. Once set and cooled, clear snap-on lids can be placed on the container, enabling the product to be seen. If the container is small containing, for example, four halves, it is a perfect individual hors-d'oeuvres, and can be marketed as such. All that is necessary for the purchaser is to remove the snap-on lid, perhaps place a small sprig of parsley on top, and place it on the dinner-party table. Sachets of aspic are readily available, and the specific instructions provided should be followed. Trade quantities are also available from manufacturers.

Winter eggs

The provision of artificial light in winter is essential if egg production is to continue without disruption.

In a small house, a 25 watt bulb is adequate for about 3 dozen birds and 40 watt for around 50. A 150 watt bulb with a reflector will be suffcient for a 20' x 10' building. Fluorescent tube lighting is also satisfactory. It is essential to incorporate a time-switch in the circuit so that the light is switched on and off automatically.

A total of 16 hours of light a day will keep egg production at satisfactory levels. Start giving extra light before dusk, gradually increasing the duration to com-

Although the Japanese strains of Coturnix laying quail are the ones most frequently used for egg production, the decorative varieties such as this Tuxedo are also good producers.

pensate for the shortening days. Similarly, as the days lengthen, gradually decrease the amount of artificial light. It is important to be consistent in turning on and switching off the light, and it is here that a pre-programmed time-switch is so valuable.

In winter, the drop in temperature imposes more demands on the metabolism so that a certain proportion of energy is needed to keep warm. Bear this in mind and, if necessary, increase the rations accordingly.

Table quail

In Britain, the same strains of Coturnix quail are used for egg production as well as for the table. In the USA, the Bobwhite is also raised for meat. Commercial battery systems and floor systems are used for rearing table birds, but the floor system is that most commonly used.

A house with a concrete floor is the most appropriate because of the dangers associated with rats which can kill adult quail with ease. Ridge ventilation in association with side windows is ideal, so that ventilation can be controlled. A very large house will probably rely on fan ventilation, but this should not be necessary if the tendency to overstock is resisted.

Many producers find that dividing a house into separate pens is better than having one large house. Quail are nervous birds and the tendency to panic and flap in one direction can lead to problems of management in this respect. An easy and relatively cheap way of sub-dividing the floor space is to use game netting. Agri-frames Ltd., for example, specialise in supplying netting and supports for making such pens. The photograph on page 34 illustrates this.

Each pen or floor space needs wood shavings litter, a suspended or gravity-fed feeder, or one which the birds cannot scratch food out of, and ideally, an automatic watering system.

Young quail will have artificial heat as described in the breeding section, and as illustrated in the photograph on page 32. A certain proportion, or indeed all the females, may be separated for future egg production, leaving the males behind for table production. The aim will be to produce quail with a liveweight of 6-7 oz at the age of 6 weeks, with a conversion ratio of around 3:1. In other words, for every three ounces of food consumed, around one ounce of weight is produced.

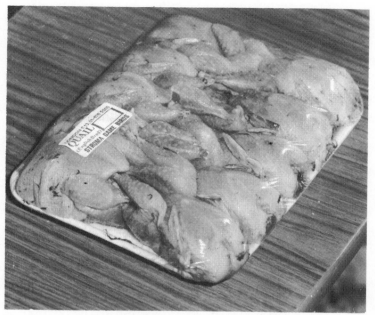

Plucked, gutted and dressed quail packaged ready for sale as fresh or frozen quail. Photograph by courtesy of Poultry World.

It is not feasible to weigh all the birds, of course, but it is a good idea to take a few sample weighings, using say half a dozen birds. This will give a general indication of the average weight of the batch.

The easiest way to weigh a quail is to use a small bag with a draw string at the top. The bird is popped into the bag, the draw strings tightened and then the whole thing is suspended on a spring balance. Those made by Salter and supplied by Elt are ideal. It takes only a moment or two, there is no distress caused to the bird, and it is released immediately after weighing. In a recent conversation with a table quail producer, she revealed to me that she used her daughter's school gym shoes bag for weighing the quail. After complaints from her daughter, she eventually made one for herself, and went to the trouble of hand embroidering a quail on it, in chain stitch!

WEIGHINGS

Take sample weighings of about six birds per batch in order to have an average weight every week until it is time to slaughter them.

KEEPING RECORDS

Everyone has their own system of keeping records. The form of it is not important. What is necessary is to ensure that all the details in relation to weight gain and feed consumed are recorded.

DATE HATCHED:			NUMBER:_____
	AVERAGE LIVEWEIGHT	FEED CONSUMED	COMMENTS
WEEK 1			
WEEK 2			
WEEK 3			
WEEK 4			
WEEK 5			
WEEK 6			
WEEK 7			
WEEK 8:			
TOTAL			LOSSES:

Those who prefer to use normal scales can utilize a polythene ice-cream carton — of the deep kind, or a cardboard shoe box. Pop in the quail and replace the lid, then place on the scales, remembering to subtract the known weight of the box from the total. Those who may feel that to use such readily available commodities is amateurish may prefer to buy a ready-made weighing cone and scales from commercial poultry suppliers.

Killing, plucking and dressing

The usual method of killing is to sever the head in one quick movement. For this, a sharp butcher's knife or cleaver used in conjunction with a wooden block is suitable, although some producers find that sharp pruning shears are effective. Alternatively, poultry equipment suppliers sell a purpose - made poultry killer which operates on a guillotine principle.

Allow the bird to bleed, but it is not necessary to hang quail as it is with other game birds. Plucking should take place as quickly as possible, and here there are several alternatives.

Dry plucking: This is quite simply the removal of the feathers without using water or any other medium to assist the process. Plucking by hand can be a rapid process for those experienced in the field, but mechanical dry plucking machines are available where large quantities are involved. Many people use these for the rough plucking, finishing off the pin feathers by hand, scraping or using a wax finish (detailed below).

Wet plucking: Here, the bled birds are immersed in scalding water for a moment then removed and plucked as soon as possible. When plucking is complete, they are immersed in chilled water to cool.

Waxing: The principle of waxing is that the birds are dipped in molten wax and as this cools and hardens, the feathers come off with the wax crust. As referred to earlier, some producers use this method as a 'finishing' technique after initial rough plucking.

Coloder powder: This is a relatively new technique using a product imported from France and distributed by Minting Farm Supplies. It is an organic product and one pack is sufficient for about 30 - 35 quail.

Once plucked, the birds are drawn. Traditionally, the innards were not removed and Mrs. Beeton would have frowned on such a practice. Modern susceptibilities however, demand that gutting is as complete as possible and commercial table quail will certainly need to be processed in this way, unless they are being sold to a butcher for processing.

Removing the neck

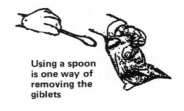

Using a spoon is one way of removing the giblets

Fold the skin over the neck end and twist the wings over to hold

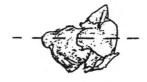

Sawing the carcase in half enables the giblets to be removed easily

Gutting is not as easy as it is with poultry, bearing in mind the relative smallness of the birds. I have found that utilising a spoon inserted in the neck end and rotating it inside the body cavity is as effective as anything. Cutting around the vent and enlarging the opening there then allows the innards to be drawn out. Some producers find this process too fiddly and time-consuming, and slit the birds down the back in order to gut them. Some complete the process by boning the birds at the same time, selling the finished product as 'boned quail'.

Once gutted, with the neck cut off close to the body and the legs cut off at the first joint up from the foot, the birds should be chilled again while awaiting packaging.

Packaging table quail

The usual way of packing quail is on polystyrene tray containers and covered with cling film sealed into position. A common procedure is to package four birds to each tray, arranged neatly, breast-side upwards. The photograph on page 71 shows ten birds packaged in this way, with a label showing the producer's name and the description that they are 'English bred quail'.

Oven-ready birds, as described above, can be sold fresh or frozen, depending on the particular market requirements. One great advantage of quail over game birds is that they are available right through the year, rather than on a seasonal basis. This is an important marketing point, in making 'game' dishes available to connoisseurs all through the year.

Smoked quail

A popular delicatessen commodity, smoked quail is definitely for the top end of the market. If an enterprise is to be expanded in this direction, the best way is to arrange a contract with a local smoking company so that they do it in batches as necessary. Smoking of food is a skilled task and as there are EEC directives with regard to safety, it is better to let a specialist company do it. The local Yellow Pages will put you in touch with appropriate companies.

The recipe section further on in the book gives details of various ways of cooking quail to good effect. When selling table quail direct to customers, as for example in a farm shop, being able to give them advice on how to cook them is important if they have not tried quail before.

Light restriction

Table quail grow more quickly and the males' sexual development is slowed down if the amount of light to them is restricted. This does not mean that they have to be kept in a twilight zone, as is the case with so many poultry broilers, but no artificial light should be made available to them, as for egg producers. Some producers, I am afraid, go to absurd lengths in blocking out the light reaching the cages. I am against this on humanitarian grounds. Every creature has a right to natural light.

Marketing

Marketing is always the difficult aspect of any enterprise, particularly where the production side may take up most of one's time. In recent years, British agriculture has become very one-sided in that the farmer has only had to think about production, leaving the marketing to a centralized body. Such a situation has led to gross over-production in some sectors, such as grain and milk, with widespread criticism of the large farming sector being subsidized by EEC subsidies, while, at the same time much of British industry has had to fend for itself.

As far as quail production is concerned, the producers have tended to be small or part-time farmers, who have not been part of the traditional farming establishment. As a result, they are far more entrepreneurial and ready to meet consumer demand.

The main demand is for quail eggs and table quail for the quality delicatessen market, although the potential sales of breeding stock should not be overlooked. The sales of ornamental breeds of quail can also provide a valuable side-line.

Local delicatessens, butchers, game dealers and hotels are obvious places to start. In fact starting on a small scale has much to recommend it. A farm shop on site is worth considering, as long as the site is in reasonable proximity to an urban or suburban area. The Farm Shop and Pick Your Own Association is worth contacting in this respect. Small local sales are also possible through local markets and the Womens' Institute markets. The appropriate addresses will be found in the Reference section.

If distribution further afield becomes a possibility — and here, production must be regular and consistent — it is important to contact specialist organisations such as Food from Britain, British Food Finds, and Good Food Retailing. The Delicatessen and Fine Foods Association is worth contacting, as well as the Institute of Grocery Distribution. Again, all the addresses will be found at the back of the book.

British Food Finds publishes an excellent directory which circulates within the trade, and enables retailers and distributors to contact producers with a view to stocking or distributing their products. All listings are free which, consequently, makes it a far more comprehensive directory than Food from Britain's directory where entries are charged. Home Farm, the journal of The Small Farmers' Association, has a very comprehensive directory called The Home Farm Source Book which is published once every three years. This circulates to the public as well as the trade and, again, listings are quite free. Just write with your details to Home Farm, whose address is given under the Bibliography on page 91.

Specializing and turning the product into a 'value-added' one will give it even more distinctive value. Reference has already been made to the production of luxury items such as quail eggs in aspic and so on. An aspect which is not often considered is to open part of the enterprise to the public, particularly if it is near an urban conurbation. A small area where different types of quail can be seen in aviary conditions, provides a source of interest. In conjunction with guided tours of the commercial production side, it can also provide a useful and educational experience for school parties. In Britain, it is common to find the rather rigid attitude that such things have nothing to do with 'real farming'. But, at a time when diversification is essential, in order to keep up with rapidly changing economic and agricultural conditions, such attitudes are not only archaic but pathetic.

On the question of diversification, it is worth knowing that the Ministry of Agriculture's ADAS (Agricultural Development Advisory Service) will provide help, advice and information free of charge. Although they have recently started charging for their services, enterprises which are regarded as being a diversification from the usual agricultural activities are not charged. The address of your nearest ADAS office will be in the local telephone directory or Yellow Pages.

Finance

For those intending to keep quail as a small business venture selling eggs, meat or breeding stock, there is the question of finance. Fortunately, setting up a quail unit is not very expensive, and it can be done on a step-by-step basis, expanding to meet demand. There are only four really big full-time quail enterprises in Britain. The others are on a smaller scale and are run on a part-time basis. There is nothing wrong with this. In fact, making use of empty farm buildings and sheds for a part-time enterprise such as this makes good economic sense. It is often a number of smaller enterprises which contribute to the success of an overall lifestyle.

As the aim is to make a profit, you need to have a detailed knowledge of all your costs. This will enable you to assess how to price your end products.

Borrowing money for expansion: The best place to begin is the bank. The manager will want to see your ideas in figures showing projected costs and sales. The very act of preparing such a plan will be useful and the bank manager's advice and experience should be helpful. Do not neglect proper insurance covering your livestock, buildings, equipment, transport etc. There are any number of companies who will provide appropriate cover and a good insurance broker should be able to help you. The English Tourist Board has a useful publication entitled 'How to Approach a Bank for Finance'. This is available from them or from The Farmshop & Pick Your Own Association. (Addresses in Reference section.)

Costs consist of fixed costs and variable costs. Fixed costs are large purchases like buildings, cages, feeders, drinkers and other things that last over a period of time. Fixed costs can spread over a period at so much per month, according to your estimate of their life and depreciation. Variable costs or running costs include everything else such as feed, transport, stock, heating etc. — in fact everything which can be regarded as a cost. Don't forget that everything that you use, particularly your car, can be assessed as a cost.

Keep careful note of all your costs in writing, including copies of all invoices that you pay. You should keep a ledger showing your sales and costs and keep it on a regular basis. You can obtain advice from your bank manager or accountant on this. You may find it easier to employ a part-time book-keeper who will keep everything in good order for a few hours work/month.

Comparative costs

Writing about relative costs is always difficult, mainly because the information goes out of date very quickly. Nevertheless, it may be useful to give one or two guidelines as to what the average cost of housing, equipment and stock were in Spring 1987. This should be regarded as general advice only. Do make your own checks before starting a quail enterprise.

Poultry house 20' x 10' suitable for housing caged units or a floor system: (The ideal is to utilize existing buildings such as barns, sheds, stables or other unused buildings)	£800—£1200
Outside extension run 20' x 10':	£130
Small house and run 8' x 4'	£175
Cages 2' x 20" x 11", including feeder	£38.50 each
Automatic drinkers	£2.60 each
Header tank	£15
Automatic drinker tubing, per 100'	£7.50
Hanging drinkers	£9.50
Hanging feeders	£8
Wood shavings, per bale	£5
Quail feed, per bag	£11/25kg
Coturnix laying quail (Good commercial strain)	£5 per bird
Ordinary Japanese/Pharoah	£3 a pair
English White	£3 a pair
American Range	£3 a pair
Tuxedo	£3 a pair
Fawn	£3 a pair
Bobwhites	£6 a pair
Chinese Painted quail	£8 a pair
Ornamental breeds, various	From £10—£200 depending on species

Health

Quail, like all living things, require good food, clean water, warm, dry and draught-free housing and regular attention. The main priority is always to prevent trouble and ill health, and to develop a ready eye for problems at an early stage. As soon as anything suspicious is noticed, such as listlessness, poor appetite, discharge from the beak or unusually coloured droppings, it is a good idea to isolate the bird immediately. This does two things; it stops the spread of possible infection to the others, and it allows the invalid a better chance of recovery. Listless birds often invite aggression and it may be severely pecked by the others.

The hospital cage

A hospital cage is a useful thing to have. This could be a wooden bird breeding cage with a wire front, or even a large cardboard box, but a cage is much better. Place some woodshavings in the bottom and clip on a feeder and drinker. The chances are that a sick bird will not be interested in the food, but it will certainly require water.

The cage should be in a warm, sheltered area, but if it is particularly cold, it may be a good idea to have a dull emitter bulb fixed up to provide a source of warmth. This can be placed outside the cage so that it is shining in sideways, through the cage front. Depending on the facilities available, it could be suspended from above. It is surprising how the provision of warmth and cosseting in this way, can sometimes make the difference between survival and loss, when all else possible has been done.

It is obviously not economic to call in the vet to see a single bird, although there is nothing to prevent you taking the cage with bird along to the vet. Where the condition is a minor one, such as a cold or simple digestive upset, it will clear up of its own accord, and the protected conditions help to make this sooner rather than later. If it is a more serious condition, there is not a lot to be done, and at least the bird will have met its end in relatively quiet comfort.

Quail chick's toes damaged by underfloor heating in a brooder.

Bacterial respiratory infections

Illnesses caused by bacteria can be treated with antibiotics, where viral ones can not. Some of the more common bacterial infections which affect the respiratory tract are bronchitis, pneumonia, infectious sinusitis and chronic respiratory disease. They all have similar symptoms of wheezing, laboured breathing, nasal discharge and loss of appetite. An antibiotic such as Neomycin administered via the drinking water can be obtained from the vet. Again, it will be seen why a hospital cage is a good idea; the dosing of the water supply is made simpler.

Bacterial digestive infections

There are several of these conditions and are detected by listlessness of the bird, lack of appetite and nature of the droppings. Enteritis results in greenish droppings. Coccidiosis also produces greenish droppings but of a more slimy nature. Again, antibiotic treatment is required and the vet will prescribe an appropriate one such as Terramycin, for dosing the drinking water.

Worms

Internal worms may be a problem with quail which are aviary housed, or which have access to the soil via pens. The importance of moving pens to fresh, clean ground on a regular basis is obvious, as well as the practice of liming aviary soil each autumn while the birds are in their winter quarters. Caged quail are very unlikely to have worm problems because they are not in a position to ingest the cysts which produce them.

Internal worms cause emaciation and loss of feather condition, and any permanent quail breeding stock which has access to the ground, should be wormed as a matter of course before being brought in for the winter. Again, it is a matter of dosing the drinking water with a vermifuge such as thiabenzole, which is available from the vet.

Scaly leg

This is a condition of the legs, where burrowing mites push up the scales of the legs and produce white encrustations. It is highly infectious and will spread rapidly to all the birds if not treated quickly. Using an old toothbrush and warm soapy water, brush off the encrustations, then dry the legs before applying benzylbenzoate which is available from the vet. This is most effective and far better than the traditional paraffin treatment.

Bumblefoot

A hard lump can sometimes form underneath the foot, where a small wound may have healed over leaving some infection behind. It is first detected when a bird is seen to be limping. If the infection is still active, the foot will feel hot and swollen and antibiotic treatment is needed. If the lump is near the surface, it can be lanced to remove the pus, then treated with any disinfectant cream.

Wounds

Any wounds such as those acquired by head banging or fighting should be cleaned and treated with antiseptic cream or disinfectant. Keep the bird in isolation until the wound has healed, in case it is pecked by the others.

Mites

Quail can be affected by mites in the same way that poultry can become infested. Proprietary insecticide powder is the answer, dusted under the wings and around the neck and rump feathers. It is available from most poultry and pet suppliers. Don't forget to dust the housing as well.

Breeding problems

Reference has already been made to the necessity of housing good breeding stock and not to interbreed closely related strains, unless you know that they are free of defects. If the introduction of females to males is carried out carefully, there is usually no problem, although it does occasionally happen that a male will refuse to accept a female. I once had a Coturnix layer who was constantly driven away by the male (she was part of a trio, and he devoted all his attentions to the other one . He would not mate with her but pecked her unmercifully. I eventually had to take her away and put her in solitary confinement. Her wounds healed and she seemed fit and healthy, with a good appetit e, when without warning she died. I have often wondered whether the male knew more than I did, and whether there is some instinctive survival method which operates with discrimination in these cases.

The only other problem which is likely to occur is that of egg binding, where a female occasionally is seen to sit for long periods of time without laying an egg. The best solution, as with other poultry, is to hold her over steam (a bowl of hot water — but take care not to drop her), and gently massage the vent with vaseline. This is really all that is possible for if the egg breaks inside her, it invariably leads to death. Although infection is usually given as the reason why death occurs, it seems to me that shock plays a major part, for a bird can die before infection has had a chance to develop.

I have already referred to possible problems with young quail. If a good level of hygiene and incubation practice is maintained, problems will be minimised. The incubator and brooder area needs complete cleaning and disinfecting after use and before a new batch of eggs and young are introduced. Most problems with poor hatches are usually connected with one of the following reasons: poor breeding stock, low fertility of parents, poor standard of nutrition in parents, infection in eggs caused by poor standards of hygiene, temperature fluctuations, humidity fluctuations, inadequate turning of the eggs.

Feather pecking

This is an old problem in the poultry world and everyone seems to have their favourite remedies, from sprinkling pepper to beak trimming. I am certainly against the latter practice on humanitarian grounds and it is rarely carried out even in Britain's commercial batteries these days. The practice has been condemned by many organisations and a recent survey in Britain showed that it has declined enormously over the last five years.

Worth trying is a relatively new product, imported from France, and called 'Stop-Pek'. It is claimed to be a completely organic product, based on pine extracts, and it is sprayed onto the birds which are being picked on. The smell is claimed to repel attackers. It is distributed in the UK by Minting Farm Supplies (See Reference section).

Notifiable diseases

Finally, quail can be affected by Newcastle disease or Fowl pest, although it is primarily found in chickens. Symptoms are paralysis of the legs and throwing the head backwards. It is a notifiable disease in Britain so the vet or local office of the Ministry of Agriculture should be notified.

Quail Recipes

It is not necessary to hang quail as it is with other game birds, merely to allow it to bleed after the head has been removed. Traditionally, the innards were not removed and Mrs. Beeton would have frowned on such a practice. Modern susceptibilities, however, demand that gutting is as complete as possible, and I have already referred to the fact that it is common commercially, for the birds to be split down the back in order to do this.

The following is a selection of recipes which you may like to try, if you have not done so before.

Mrs Beeton's recipe

Ingredients: Quails, butter, toast.
Method: These birds keep good several days and should be roasted without drawing (but not if you have modern susceptibilities — see above). Truss them with the legs close to the body, and the feet pressing upon the thighs. Place some slices of toast in the dripping pan, allowing a piece of toast for each bird. Roast for 15-20 minutes; keep them well basted and serve on the toast.

Quick roast quail

This is my favourite way of cooking them and the bacon adds to the flavour, as well as preventing too much drying.
Ingredients: Quail, 2 slices of bacon per bird.
Method: Wrap up each bird in the bacon and use wooden sausage sticks to keep them in place. Roast in a medium oven for about 20 minutes and serve with any of the sauces or garnishes normally used with chicken or game.

Grilled quail

Ingredients: Quail, butter, lemon juice, bacon slices, salt and black pepper, breadcrumbs.
Method: Slit each quail down the backbone. (A strong pair of scissors is adequate for this.) Flatten each side and sprinkle with lemon juice, salt and pepper. Dip in melted butter and roll in breadcrumbs. Grill for about 5-6 minutes on each side. Meanwhile, roll up the bacon slices and grill them for the last few minutes with the quail.

Serve quail with bacon rolls and garnish with mushrooms.

French roast quail

Ingredients: Quail, butter, vine leaves, toast, salt, black pepper, milk.
Method: Wipe quail inside and out. Place in a saucepan with just enough milk to cover them. Simmer gently for 6-7 minutes. Remove and put the saucepan and its contents to one side for the moment.

Smear the quail with butter and wrap them in vine leaves. Sprinkle with salt and pepper and place in a buttered oven-proof dish. Roast for 10 minutes in a medium oven, then take the dish out of the oven. Strain the contents of the saucepan and pour over the quail. Replace the dish in the oven and cook for another 10 minutes.

Serve each quail on a slice of toast and garnish with wedges of lemon and sprigs of parsley.

APPENDIX 1

A further word about cages

My dislike of battery cages is well known, particularly where the system is abused and they are overstocked. I feel that it is essential to keep livestock as humanely as possible, with due regard to their natural inclinations. This is not to imply that birds which are given access to the outside are necessarily better looked after than those inside. Some of the worst cases of abuse have been where poultry or other birds have been left huddled and shivering in a quagmire of mud, in what the owners have euphemistically called 'free-range conditions'.

Quail need to be confined for their own protection and for the owner's peace of mind. If they are being kept for commercial purposes, the system of management needs to be one which is realistic and economic as well as humane. The battery system is the most economic and practicable one for the large scale producer, and where it is not abused, it can also be one of the most humane. In case you think that this is a contradiction in terms, I shall describe the practice of at least one commercial producer in the UK who uses them.

The cages supplied by Curfew, which I have referred to earlier, are 20" x 24" x 11" high. Each cage comes fitted with a feeder, and manually filled or automatic drinkers are easily fitted. The floor is plastic covered mesh which is easy on the feet, and eggs as they are laid, roll forward for collection. The cages can be stacked four or five high and there is a removable droppings tray beneath each one.

Each cage, in theory, can hold 15 quail, but it is not necessary to have as many as that. In summer, each cage can be lifted out quite easily and placed on grass in a sheltered area so that the quail have access to the grass which comes up through the mesh.

One producer I met does this regularly, placing her 30 cages outside, on a different area each day so that it keeps down the grass in her adjoining field. The cages have a windbreak in the form of a line of straw bales placed in the way of the prevailing wind. If the weather is particularly windy, cold or wet, the cages are left inside. This practice, according to the owner, is a reasonable compromise, for she shares my dislike of batteries in general, but can see the value of them if used with a little imagination. The supplier of the cages confirmed that several producers use his cages in this way; adding that most quail producers are in fact, small scale, and prefer to utilise small scale practices.

APPENDIX 11   A Miscellany of quail

QUAIL

Short and plump,
Timid but inquisitive;
Dull but pretty,
Not very clever,
But a long way from silly.

— **Alex Smith**

'No quailing, Mrs Gaskell! No drawing back!'

— **Letter from the Reverend Patrick Bronte to Ellen Nussey, 1855, referring to Mrs Gaskell's undertaking to write the life of Charlotte Bronte.**

'Are they birds of prey?'
'No, they're partridges.'

— **Two ladies examining a display of quail at the Ardingly Show, 1986.**

English: Quail
French: La caille
Welsh: Sofliar

 is for quaint, quiet, quarantined, quarrelsome, quavering, quivering, queer, querulous, questing, questioning, queueing, quibbling, quick, quipping, quizzing, quoting, quelling, quixotic, quaility QUAIL !

Reference section

Bibliography

QUAIL: THEIR BREEDING AND MANAGEMENT. G.E.S. Robbins. World Pheasant Association 1984 (UK).

QUAIL MANUAL. Albert F. Marsh. Marsh Farm Publications. 1976 (USA)

RAISING BOBWHITE QUAIL FOR COMMERCIAL USE. Circular 514. Clemson University & U.S. Department of Agriculture. 1964 (USA).

THAT QUAIL, ROBERT. Margaret Stranger. J.B. Lippincott Co. 1966 (USA). Hodder & Stoughton. 1967 (UK).

ORNAMENTAL BIRDS. Stanislav Chvapil. Hamlyn. 1983. (UK).

PART-TIME FARMING. Katie Thear. Ward Lock. 1983 (UK).

THE FAMILY SMALLHOLDING. Katie Thear. B. T. Batsford. 1983 (UK).

A KIND OF LIVING. Katie Thear. Hamish Hamilton/Channel 4 TV. 1984. (UK).

HOME FARM, journal of The Small Farmers' Association, Broad Leys Publishing Co., Widdington, Saffron Walden, Essex CB11 3SP. Tel: (0799) 40922 — Britain's small farming journal, with regular articles on quail and other poultry. £8 per annum.

FANCY FOWL, Crondall Cottage, Highclere, Newbury, Berks. — Magazine for poultry fanciers.

POULTRY WORLD, Carew House, Wallington, Surrey SM6 0DX — Magazine for intensive poultry industry.

CAGE AND AVIARY BIRDS, Prospect House, 9-13 Ewell Road, Cheam, Sutton, Surrey, SM1 4QQ. Tel: 01 661 4300 — Newspaper for cage and aviary bird enthusiasts.

Breeders and equipment suppliers

CURFEW COTURNIX QUAIL, Buttons Hill, Southminster Road, Althorne, Essex CM3 6EN. Tel: (0621) 741923 — Breeders of 'Crusader' strain commercial Coturnix quail. Suppliers of purpose-made quail cages, brooders, drinkers, feeders, header tanks and automatic watering systems. Also, a wide range of incubators.

FAYRE GAME, Lodge Lane Nurseries, Lodge Lane, Lytham, Lancashire FY8 5RP. Tel: (0253) 738640 — Breeders of Japanese, English White, American Range, Tuxedo, Fawn Coturnix strains, and Bobwhites.

MOYLE M.O. LTD., Lairds Cottage, Burradon, Thropton, Morpeth, Northumberland. Tel: Rothbury 30202 — Breeders of Japanese, English White, American Range, Tuxedo and Fawn Coturnix quail.

PHILIPS & HEATH, Brook Cottage Aviaries, Broughhall, Whitchurch, Shropshire. Tel: (0948) 2651 — Chinese Painted quail, Japanese, Bobwhite, Californians.

BROOKSIDE AVIARIES, Stream Farm, Wilmington, Polegate, East Sussex. Tel: (032 12) 2358 — Small quail houses for use in aviaries, Chinese Painted quail and silver variety, Bobwhites.

GRANGE AVIARIES & PET CENTRE, Woodhouse Lane, Botley, Southampton. Tel: (04892) 81260 — Complete aviaries, Twilweld netting and aviary panels, various varieties of Coturnix quail.

SOUTHERN AVIARIES, Brookhouse Farm, Tinkers Lane, Hadlow Down, Uckfield, East Sussex TN22 4EU. Tel: (082585) 283. — Wide range of aviaries and associated equipment.

NEWMARKET AVIARIES, Newmarket Lane, Clay Lane, Clay Cross, Chesterfield, Derbyshire. Tel: (0246) 863506 — Chinese Painted quail, Bobwhites.

MICHAEL SUMMERLIN, Quest Cottage, 34 Hatherop, Cirencester, Glos. Tel: Coln St Aldwyns 281 — Breeder of ornamental quail including Californian quail, Gambel's quail, Scaled quail, Elegant quail, Mountain quail, Harlequin quail, Rain quail, Bobwhite quail, Masked Bobwhite, Crested Bobwhite and Japanese quail.

Quail producers

FAYRE GAME (address as above) — Whole or boned quail, fresh or frozen. Also smoked quail and fresh quail eggs.

PARK HILL PRODUCE, Park Hill, Appledore, Ashford, Kent TN26 2BJ Tel: (023 383) 201 — Aviary reared fresh quail and fresh quail eggs.

QUALITY QUAIL, Hazelhurst, Weare, Axbridge, Somerset BS26 2ND. Tel: (0934) 712619 — Fresh, frozen or smoked quail and hard-boiled eggs.

SHERSTON QUAIL, St. Catherines, Sherston, Malmesbury, Wilts. SN16 0NN. Tel: (0666) 840387 — fresh or frozen quail, pickled eggs.

J & S WILSON, Culcombe Farm, Monksilver, Taunton, Somerset TA4 4JG. Tel: (0984) 56323 — Fresh or frozen quail.

A & F WOOD, Redlynch Farm, Redlynch, Bruton, Somerset. BA10 0NW. Tel: (0749) 812761 — Fresh or frozen quail and quail eggs.

COSTA & CO LTD., Staffordshire Street, London SE15 — Importers and distributors of boiled French quail eggs.

CLEMENTS FARM, The Old Thatch, Crawley, Winchester, Hants. SO21 2PR. Tel: (0962) 72327 — Fresh quail eggs.

ISIS FISH FARM, Eynsham Mill, Oxford OX8 1EJ. Tel: (0865) 881751 — Fresh quail eggs.

NEWTON HALL QUAIL, Malpas, Cheshire. Tel: (0948) 860544 — Fresh, frozen and smoked quail, fresh quail eggs.

D & M PAUL, Ivory Farmhouse, Burghclere, Newbury, Berks. RG15 9LP. Tel: (0635) 27362 — Fresh quail eggs.

ASHDOWN SMOKERS, Skellerah Farm, Corney, Near Millom, Cumbria LA19 5TW. Tel: (06578) 324 — Smoked quail and smoked/spiced quail eggs.

SUFFOLK SMOKED FOODS, Reapers Cottage, Lower Raydon, Ipswich, Suffolk IP7 5QQ. Tel: (0473) 822629 — Smoked quail. Will also undertake to smoke customers' own produce on a contractual basis.

THAMES VALLEY EGGS LTD., Membury, Lambourn Woodlands, Newbury, Berks. RG16 7TX. Tel: (0488) 71101 — Fresh quail eggs.

GOLDESBOROUGH QUAILS, 44 Standard Way, Fareham Industrial Park, Fareham, Hants. PO16 8XD. Tel: (0329) 238321 — Fresh and frozen quail, fresh and pickled quail eggs.

MINOLA SMOKED PRODUCTS, Kencot Hill Farm House, Filkins, Lechlade, Glos GL7 3QY. Tel:(036 786) 391 — Smoked and fresh quail eggs. Also smoked quail.

CURFEW COTURNIX QUAIL (address as above) — Fresh, frozen and smoked quail. Fresh quail eggs.

Organisations

SMALL FARMERS' ASSOCIATION, PO Box 71, Thames House, 1-4 Queen Street Place, London EC4R 1JA.

BRITISH POULTRY FEDERATION LTD., 52-54 High Holborn, London WC1 6SX. Tel: 01 242 4683.

BRITISH POULTRY BREEDERS & HATCHERIES ASSOCIATION (address as for British Poultry Federation).

DELICATESSEN AND FINE FOODS ASSOCIATION, 6 The Broadway, Thatcham, Berks RG13 4JA. Tel: (0635) 69033.

INSTITUTE OF GROCERY DISTRIBUTION, Letchmore Heath, Watford, Herts. WD2 8DQ. Tel: (09276) 7141.

NATIONAL FEDERATION OF WOMEN'S INSTITUTES, Markets Advisor, 39 Eccleston Street, London SW1 9NT. Tel: 01 730 7212.

GOOD FOOD RETAILING, Dewberry Millpark Ltd., 161-165 Greenwich High Road, Greenwich, London SE10 8JA. Tel: 01 853 5444.

FOOD FROM BRITAIN, 301-344 Market Towers, New Covent Garden Market, 1 Nine Elms Lane, London SW8 5NQ. Tel: 01 720 2144.

FARM SHOP & PICK YOUR OWN ASSOCIATION, Hunger Lane, Muggington, Derby DE6 4PL. Tel: (0332) 360 991.

Miscellaneous

MINTING FARM SUPPLIES LTD., Minting, Horncastle, Lincolnshire LN9 5RX, Tel:(065 887) 220.

BRINSEA INCUBATORS, Dept 56, Station Road, Sandford, Avon BS19 5RA. Tel: (0934) 823039.

THE DOMESTIC FOWL TRUST, Honeybourne Pastures, Honeybourne, Evesham, Worcs WR11 5QJ. Tel: (0386) 833038.

AGRIFRAMES GAME PROTECTION LTD., Charlwoods Road, East Grinstead, Sussex RH19 2HG. Tel: (0342) 28649.

GEORGE H. ELT LTD., Eltex Works, Bromyard Road, Worcester WR2 Tel: (0905) 422377.

BRITISH FOOD FINDS, Rich & Green Ltd., 5 Luke Street, London EC2. Tel: 01 729 4822.

WALNER WILDFOWL & POULTRY HOUSING, Wyan, Stoke Rivers, Barnstaple, North Devon EX32 7LD.

NEWBRIDGE FARM PRODUCTS, Aylton, Ledbury, Herefordshire. Tel: (053 183) 276.

WOODLAND WAYS HOUSING. Elm House, Main Road, Saltfleetby, Louth, Lincolnshire. Tel: (050 783) 230.

SMALLHOLDING & FARM SUPPLY CO., Gerard Street, Sheffield S8 9SJ. Tel: (0742) 587845.

GARDENCRAFT HOUSING, Farmers Yard, Tremadog, Porthmadog, Gwynedd LL49 9RD. Tel: (0766) 3036.

PINTAFEN LTD., 93 Hospital Raod, Bury St. Edmunds, Suffolk IP33 3LH. Tel: (0284) 2828.

F.W. PERKINS POULTRY EQUIPMENT, Unit 17, Finnimore Trading Estate, Ottery St. Mary, Devon EX11 1NR. Tel: (040 481) 2605.

AUTONEST LTD., Brampton Wood Lane, Desborough, Northants NN14 2SR. Tel: Kettering 760 332.

MARDLE PRODUCTS INCUBATORS, 22 Market Street, Buckfastleigh, Devon TQ11 0BA. Tel: (0364) 43441.

United States of America

MARSH FARMS, 14232 Brookhurst Street, Garden Grove, California 92643.

Index